PASTORAL PREACHING

PASTORAL PREACHING

Timeless Truth for Changing Needs

GARY D. STRATMAN

Abingdon Press
Nashville

Pastoral Preaching: Timeless Truth for Changing Needs

Copyright © 1983 by Abingdon Press

Library of Congress Cataloging in Publication Data

STRATMAN, GARY D., 1946–
    Pastoral preaching.
    Bibliography: p.
    1. Preaching. I. Title.
    BV4211.2.S83   1982   251   82-16373
ISBN 0-687-30139-4

MANUFACTURED BY THE PARTHENON PRESS AT
NASHVILLE, TENNESSEE, UNITED STATES OF AMERICA

— ACKNOWLEDGMENTS —

This project owes much to many. Wherever possible I have cited those who have challenged and sharpened my understanding of pastoral preaching. Not all could be called by name. For there have been those in two congregations who have demonstrated that the whole body of Christ is involved in pastoring the flock and proclaiming the Word. These are the undershepherds of Jesus Christ.

A special word of gratitude is due Professors Peggy Way, John Killinger, and Liston Mills for their constructive criticism and advice. Ms. Kay Scranton provided help above and beyond the call of duty in typing the manuscript through its many stages.

Yet none of this would have even been attempted had it not been for my wife, Deborah Gable Stratman. It was her encouragement and patience that created an atmosphere in which this work could be completed.

CONTENTS

———— INTRODUCTION ————

There is a genuine hunger for pastoral preaching. People who are surrounded by the impersonal world of news bulletins, federal guidelines, and "medical research" long for truth which comes through a person who cares about them. The pastor (shepherd of souls) who demonstrates over time concern for people will elicit a hearing. But a hearing for what? The hunger is for more than personal counseling from the pulpit. Unfortunately "pastoral preaching" has become identified exclusively with a problem-solving format. A sermon of this type moves from a vexing personal problem to a psychologically sound "Christian" answer. This style often sacrifices the deeper insight of the Bible by not wrestling with a text of scripture until the Word of God comes through. Also a preaching plan based on urgent personal problems reduces "our canon" of Holy Scripture. The "whole counsel of God" becomes less than that when preachers avoid large portions of the Bible over a period of several years.

The purpose of this book is to develop and demonstrate an approach to preaching that is responsive to human need without sacrificing the pastoral responsibility of speaking over time from "the whole counsel of God." "For I did not shrink from declaring to you the whole counsel of God. Take heed to yourselves and to all the flock, in which the Holy Spirit has made you overseers, to care for the church of God which he obtained with the blood of his own Son" (Acts 20:27-28).

How are we to go beyond the limitations of "preaching as counseling or problem solving" and still speak to the deepest needs of people? This question is the focus of my first chapter. This chapter does not offer a novel answer to this question, or repudiate the concept of pastoral preaching. What is offered is a corrective. An inadequate interpretation of the term "pastoral" must be corrected before the practice of preaching

9

is significantly altered. A fuller, richer understanding of "pastor" emerges only when we dig deeply into the biblical image of "shepherd." My contention (spelled out in chapter 2) is that shepherding involves a pastoral community that deals with the personal *and* the social, acceptance *and* judgment, healing *and* teaching. This broader biblical view of shepherding has tremendous implications for preaching.

The third chapter demonstrates that prayerful yet critical study of biblical texts done for and with a congregation is a pastoral act. In following a balanced course of biblical lessons such as the three-year lectionary, preaching can speak to "life situations" by sensitive listening to text and people. The very idea of following a lectionary has often been seen as a polar extreme to "pastoral preaching." Hopefully the lectionary may come to be seen as a helpful tool in doing the work of the pastor.

Chapters 4 and 5 are concerned with providing some demonstration of the movement from pastoral theology to praxis. This movement is seen in the unrelenting but crucial task of sermon preparation and delivery. The suggestions for indirect and direct sermon preparation plus the three sample sermons are not presented as models. Rather they are illustrations of one pastor's attempts to bring a shepherding perspective to preaching.

The final chapter is an annotated bibliography on pastoral preaching. In my research I found no substantial bibliography on the subject. The one presented in chapter 6 is done with the hope that it will help open up discussion, research, and development of pastoral approaches to preaching.

CHAPTER I

Pastoral Preaching: The Truth in Love

"There's just one reason, you know, why I come dragging in here every Sunday. I want to find out if the whole thing's true." "Just true," she said. "That's all. Either it is or it isn't and that's the one question you avoid like death."

—Rooney to her pastor-friend Rev. Nicolet
in *The Final Beast*[1]

It is no news that we have recently gone through a period when preaching was especially suspect. Marshall McLuhan questioned our assumptions about communication, and theologians wondered out loud over our "God talk." "The death of preaching" invited hastily assembled articles and seminars. Today the question is no longer, Will preaching survive the twentieth century? but, How then shall we preach? Many of us caught up in the "alternatives" of a few years ago are now seeking to preach faithfully the enduring word of the gospel. This renewed interest in preaching draws heat and light from the embers of a "gospel truth" which outlasts our fads and factions. Despite our periodic gloom not all pulpits become empty hearths. There are flickering reminders that truly biblical preaching speaks a searing, saving word to social issues as well as to personal needs. Much more frightening to me than the "death of preaching" is the discovery that

11

preaching is ". . . that divine, saving activity in history, which began two thousand years ago in the advent of Christ and in His personal relationships with men and women, and has continued throughout the ages in the sphere of redeemed personal relationships. . . ."[2] The fearsome prospect is not that preaching is an outmoded form of communication. Rather in what appears to be utter foolishness, preaching is the means of God's saving activity in the world. Now *that* should bring a holy fear over the one who preaches.

The Preacher's Dilemma

Since moving from a teaching and counseling ministry into the parish as a pastor I have found myself in a real dilemma. Every pastor faces the problem of preaching to those caught up in what P. T. Forsyth called, "the press and care of life." How am I to preach to people who want to know if the incredible Good News is true? Rooney, the young woman who confronts her pastor in *The Final Beast,* wants more than an honest opinion. She is seeking the truth. What's more, on many gray-tinged Sunday mornings she seeks it through a very human, fallible preacher. Knowing his humanness does not keep her from crying out in inexplicable anger for a true Word. Perhaps the anger was the sound of "quiet desperation" breaking the surface.

"Dilemma" is too weak a word for the place one stands between a "Rooney's desperation" and the mysteries of God's grace. Yet that is the place where the pastor-preacher must stand. Phillips Brooks understood this necessary dilemma. Preaching for Brooks included two essential elements: truth and personality. Neither of the two elements should be neglected in Christian preaching: "Christianity is Christ; and we can easily understand how a truth which is of such peculiar character that a person can stand forth and say of it 'I am the Truth,' must always be best conveyed through, must indeed be almost incapable of being perfectly conveyed except through personality."[3]

The quotation above was selected because Brooks' more epigrammatic statement, "preaching is the bringing of truth through personality" is memorable but often misleading. The Christian pulpit has frequently been more noted for personality than truth. Perhaps this is because we have not taken seriously what Brooks meant by personality. "Truth through personality" has often meant only the personal persuasiveness, attractiveness, "charisma," or power of the speaker. We think of the cult of personality which can so quickly form around a Henry Ward Beecher, an Aimee Semple McPherson, or the preacher who packs them in down at Old First Church.

The second misunderstanding of "preaching as truth through personality" is seen in an unhealthy emphasis on the preacher as personality theorist. This kind of preaching is often marked by an adroit description of the inner working of human personality, with some attempt at a prescription as well. The preacher's personality should not be ignored or denied, also the pastor-preacher needs an understanding of human personality. Yet the accent can rest too heavily on these elements.

"Personality" for Brooks rested on his theological understanding of the incarnation. The truth could only be known in one who could say, "I am the Truth." That truth of God has come in human personality and continues to be reborn in and through human personalities who respond to the living Christ. Truth through personality is the continuation of Christ's work in the world. "As my Father has sent me, even so I send you" (John 20:21). It is in discovering *how* we are sent to proclaim the gospel that we discover how we can dare to stand as utterly human, fallible bearers of the truth. Being sent as Jesus was sent means not hiding or denying our humanity but "taking the form of a servant" (Phil. 2:7). The continuing paradox is that as we empty ourselves of any pretentions of power and stand before our sisters and brothers as an all too earthen vessel the transcendent power of God's Word is free to do its saving work:

We are no better than pots of earthenware to contain this treasure, and this proves that such transcendent power does not come from us, but is God's alone. Hard-pressed on every side, we are never hemmed in; bewildered, we are never at our wits' end; hunted, we are never abandoned to our fate; struck down, we are not left to die.

(II Cor. 4:7-9 NEB)

In owning up to feelings of being "hard-pressed . . . bewildered . . . hunted," one becomes more sensitive to the social-personal needs of those who come seeking assurance that they are not "abandoned . . . struck down . . . left to die." The transcendent power of a living Word which confronts, heals, demands, saves is not the product of my sensitivity or insight. Personality is not a replacement but a vehicle for truth. There is the danger in "person-centered" preaching for the Christian faith to be seen "more as medicine to be *prescribed* than as a Gospel to be *proclaimed*."[4] The preacher must be a truth teller. He or she pursues the truth through the diligent and prayerful study of the Scripture. The telling then increasingly reflects the "whole counsel of God," as God has been and is revealed in history. Charm, charisma, insight into human personality, will not replace telling "the gospel truth."

But to preach the Gospel is not just to tell the truth but to tell the truth in love, and to tell the truth in love means to tell it with concern not only for the truth that is being told but with concern also for the people it is being told to. . . . Who are they? What is going on inside them? What is happening behind their faces where they have cut themselves to make them strain to hear the truth, if it is told?[5]

Here the novelist/preacher who through Rooney's lips cried out for truth, now reminds us that truth penetrates the human heart by love. No matter how hard or blunt the truth, it can be delivered in love. Indeed speaking the truth is an act of love; which demands an unflinching search for truth and an unwavering concern for its hearers.

Knowing that this is the way we are sent out to proclaim the gospel, we need, not a moratorium on the dangerous task of preaching, but a model. What picture or image captures for us the twin pulls of human need and the gospel? I do not have a new image to offer. What is offered here is an old image, that of shepherd or pastor. Perhaps this image may lead us to a new or renewed vision of preaching. *"In other words, preaching is essentially a pastoral activity.* It is part of a pastoral relationship, one activity of a settled and continuous ministry."[6]

The Need for Pastoral Preaching

Le Curé de Torey's words to the young priest in Bernanos' novel pushes us beyond a superficial understanding of "speaking to people's need":

Comforting truths, they call it! Truth is meant to save you first, and the comfort comes afterwards. Besides you've no right to call that sort of thing comfort. Might as well talk about condolences! The Word of God is a red hot iron. . . . I mean that when the Lord has drawn from me some word for the good of souls, I know, because of the pain of it.[7]

Here is a strength that is grounded in a passion for truth and a compassion for those entrusted to the pastor's care. Both are costly. A truly pastoral preaching will know the pain that the Curé speaks of in this passage. Nonetheless it is this kind of pastoral preaching that is so needed today.

Pastoral preaching has often been seen as one type of preaching among others. It has been "problem oriented," tending toward comforting truths instead of the comfort which includes demand as well as succor. "I do not believe that God ever comes livingly to a man or woman without making a claim or a demand. Nor does He ever come without proffering strength and succor. The two, the demand and the succor, are inseparably one."[8] The wholeness of the Christian faith comes through when one preaches over a year's time not on a few favorite comforting texts, or on pressing problems, but on texts that allow comfort, demand, strength, and judgment to speak from within the *full* biblical witness. In wrestling with the needs of the people (including the preacher's) and the text, a "word for the good of the souls" comes forth . . . but not painlessly.

The first step in "getting a handle" on this project has been a review of the available literature on pastoral preaching. (See the annotated bibliography, page 86.) The literature of the past thirty years has been greatly influenced by an understanding of "preaching as counseling on a group scale" and pastoring or shepherding as "tender and solicitous concern."[9] Both of these viewpoints have been very positive influences on the pastoral ministry in America, but they also have limited our understanding of pastoral preaching. Many of the books and articles dealing with pastoral preaching written from the 1940s to the 1960s were heavily influenced by Harry Emerson Fosdick's view of preaching as counseling. There is of course good reason for this. Dr. Fosdick's name continues to be a symbol of powerful preaching that ministers to individual needs, yet takes on the social, political, as well as theological issues of the day. One hundred years after his birth the need for this kind of preaching has never been greater, and the forces martialed against it never stronger.

It is, however, *not* my intent to write another book on Harry Emerson Fosdick's counseling approach to preaching. What is germane to my topic is the direction pastoral preaching has taken since Fosdick. It has been characterized by beginning a sermon with "a life-situation" problem, which is then answered by the resources of the Christian faith. Although Fosdick spoke against "topical preaching," his imitators have established a popular pattern of counseling-oriented preaching that follows a topical sermon format. This subsequent problem-centered "counseling" approach reflects an inadequate conception of the word "pastoral." There is much in addition to counseling that is a part of the pastoral perspective.

This pastoral perspective, which Seward Hiltner correctly calls "shepherding," has its roots in the Bible. Hiltner's view of shepherding has been a powerful factor in the shaping of pastoral theology in the past three decades. It has also contributed significantly to what has been called "pastoral preaching." Every facet of shepherding, according to Dr. Hiltner, should exhibit tender concern: "The Christian metaphor refers to the solicitous and tender and individualized care by the shepherd of the sheep."[10] We are to act as undershepherds of Christ, preaching and healing in his name (Mark 3:14-15). The "individualized" element does not exclude relating to small groups or even the entire congregation at one time in a pastoral manner. Rather, following Jesus' example, he would see the pastor as sensitive to the needs of the individual even in group settings. This must have been an important aspect of Jesus' ministry for the Gospel writers graphically portray the importance of the individual in the crowd. Individuals cared for by Jesus emerge from the faceless mass: the woman who touched his coat, Zacchaeus perched in the tree, and many others. Not only was he able to see pastorally, he also could have compassion for the multitude that looked for all the world like sheep without a shepherd (Mark 6:34).

We must be careful, however, that this shepherding model based on the One who is the Shepherd and Guardian of our souls (I Pet. 2:25) does not imperceptibly change foundations. The metaphor can be related to, but not founded on modern theories of counseling. For to be undershepherds of the chief Shepherd (I Pet. 5:4) calls forth a quality of love that goes beyond psychologist Carl Rogers' "unconditional positive regard." We are compelled to go beyond all such foundations to the unique sacrificial love of the "Good Shepherd." Likewise, individualized care is not synonymous with personal counseling. Beginning with the Old Testament we must develop a richer understanding of shepherding to see how Jesus is the perfect manifestation and model of the Shepherd God of Israel.

———— CHAPTER II ————

The Biblical Image of Shepherd

A predominantly rural people, the Jews reflected their nomadic history by picturing their heroes and their God in the image of a shepherd. If we dwell on the familiar, "The Lord is *my* shepherd . . . ," we miss the equally important Old Testament emphasis of a God who shepherded all his people (Ps. 80:1). In remembering this we can see the Messiah as one who came to shepherd "my people Israel" (Matt. 2:6). Jesus as the Christ is seen then not only as "personal savior" but also as the founder of a new and universal community in the New Israel. Salvation: the bringing of deliverance, healing, positive and peaceful rule, is certainly attributed to the Shepherd God in the Old Testament (Ezek. 34:15-31). It is Jesus who personifies the shepherd-savior laying down his life for the sheep (John 10:11).

Also the very root of the Hebrew word for shepherd is *raah* "from the verb 'to feed' meaning also 'to guide' and is occasionally used in reference to teaching."[1] We cannot understand the image of God as *raah* unless we see ourselves as people who have been guided, guarded, and fed by the Divine Shepherd. The evidence was in the experience of Israel, reinforced by stories, poems, and songs of the God who not only saves but nurtures. Their bodies were nourished by manna in the wilderness. Their souls hungered for and were fed by the Torah . . . Yahweh's teaching. So it is that Jesus embodies the Shepherd God's compassionate feeding of a hungry multitude, and with the same compassion is moved to teach those who are shepherdless (Mark 6:34).

The biblical metaphor of shepherd is incomplete unless the One, who saves and feeds, is also seen as the One who judges. The care of the shepherd is not only tender and solicitous but also just and sovereign. These are not traits at war within one nature. Nor does the tender, caring, accepting Shepherd God come to save us from the terrible wrath of the divine Judge. We are judged by the standards of sacrificial love, caring concern, and guardianship of the weaker brother and sister. "His judgment condemns those who shoulder aside the weaker members of the flock, but the harshest sentence falls upon unworthy shepherds who prey upon the sheep, intent upon their own comfort. Because they have exploited the helpless, God will remove them (Ezekiel 34:1-10). The awesome righteousness of the divine Shepherd requires judgment."[2]

Indeed, Jesus as the Messiah was seen by the Christian church as the direct image of the Shepherd God who will feed, gather, and lead his flock (Isa. 40:11). But this same Jesus in bearing the impress of the Shepherd God was also seen as Judge. As in the Old Testament (i.e., Ezek. 34) the Shepherd judges "between sheep and sheep." Again it is the compassion for the weak, poor, and oppressed that brings judgment from the mouth of Christ for those who have not ministered to the "least of these" (Matt. 25:31-46).

It is this image of the righteous judge that brings us back again to the shepherd as savior. For the Good Shepherd does not stand far off as a judge only, but is also the Lamb of God who fully identifies himself with the sheep. In the New Testament Jesus fulfills the vision of the Shepherd God who knows and cares for his sheep, disciplines and judges them, but also is "the Lamb of God, who takes away the sin of the world" (John 1:29). We must agree with the opinion that this mixing of metaphors (sheep-shepherd) is highly significant.[3]

As we shall see later it keeps us as undershepherds from seeing ourselves as superior to all others who are the "sheep of his hand." It also is a constant reminder that we too are called to a life of dangerous service. We are sent out "as sheep in the midst of wolves." Even as we are called to pastoral office and seek to preach, counsel, and lead we are not exempt from the pain and sacrifice of the Shepherd-Lamb.

Essential Elements of "Shepherding"

Indeed it is the fullness of the shepherding perspective that allows clergy and laypeople alike to rediscover our identity as a pastoral community. In the most thorough study of the biblical concept of shepherding that I am aware of David Steere lists the following as essential elements of this model:

I. A positive pattern of action meeting need
II. A negative pattern of action constituting a withdrawal of the first
III. A sacrificial expenditure of life
IV. Love as spontaneous, creative, and initiating[4]

It takes only a quick glance at this list to realize that our modern understanding of pastoral counseling and preaching has relied heavily on the first and last elements with a consistent disregard for the two in the middle. This has resulted in a weakening of the pastoral perspective. All four points listed here must be in constant interplay with one another so that the shepherding mission of the church does not become a weak "religious" imitation of current psychological or sociological theories. "Love as spontaneous, creative, and initiating" is the heart and soul of pastoral concern. Yet the depth that it draws from to free people from indifference and alienation is the "sacrificial expenditure of life." The acceptance of a man or woman desperately in need of acceptance does not come from a benign tolerance. It is radical acceptance that we experience in the grace of God, whose love seeks us out "while we were yet sinners." The sign of that costly acceptance is the Good Shepherd who sacrifices his life for the sheep. We cannot speak of the "unconditional love" and acceptance which God lavishes on every man and woman without knowing also that this love calls forth nothing less than "the sacrificial expenditure of life."

Often we have defined the pastoral ministry in terms of meeting human needs with positive empathetic action. Pastoral theology applied to counseling and preaching has, however, been unwilling to deal with what Dr. Steere lists as the second aspect of shepherding. Hiltner, for instance, gives only brief mention to the element of judgment in shepherding and seems to downplay its importance.[5] A survey of the literature of pastoral theology related to preaching (see annotated bibliography) will show how often the reality of personal and social sin, responsibility of choices made, the need of repentance are viewed as "unpastoral topics." They are seen as elements of a judgmental message that doesn't facilitate human growth and freedom. Of course pastoral care can become judgmental. Yet judgment, responsibility, discipline, are a part of God's love as evidenced by the shepherd who cares for the sheep. Judgment is seen as a part of the biblical concept of shepherding: ". . . God's support is withdrawn and the flock is scattered, judgment is made between the sheep, unworthy shepherds are condemned, etc."[6] While drawing this side of the pastoral perspective from the Bible, Steere is careful to place it within the framework of God's love and eschatological purposes. The withdrawal is never final, unlimited forgiveness is always present. It becomes operative when positive care can be received.[7]

If this element of shepherding is not present, the pastoral counselor never confronts irresponsible behavior, the pastoral preacher shies away from any notes of judgment, and church discipline becomes a historic relic. As long as the pastor realizes that she or he also stands under the judgment of the Good Shepherd who alone separates the sheep and goats, there is the possibility for judgment to lead to healing. Steere's emphasis has another very practical application. One of my needs that can get in the way of effective counseling and preaching is the strong desire to be successful. The wisdom of the shepherd's perspective is that there is a time for a withdrawal of our pastoral action. This does not mean a withdrawal of love and concern, but actual counseling or intervention may need to be withdrawn in working with an individual or couple. We may have to admit to ourselves and the person or persons in need that we are not getting anywhere. The pastor cannot force or coerce another person to change, or resolve problems. Not all needs can be met through pastoral action. In fact my refusal to withdraw pastorally from a counseling situation may say more about my need to be successful, to achieve "a sense of closure" than it speaks of sensitivity to the other's need.

Jesus as shepherd often displayed a remarkable sense of timing when withdrawal needed to be a part of the pastoral rhythm. Jesus knew that his physical presence could sometimes be a hindrance as people struggled with what their own response to the gospel must be. His timely withdrawal said, "It is good that I go, I must leave so that you will understand." In his final leaving he promised that the Comforter would come. Sometimes in our withdrawing we provide space for the Spirit to work—to convict us of sin, to point to the promise of forgiveness. This may have to happen in solitude or through rather unlikely "priests." As pastoral counselors we can be too available, too present, attempting to be indispensable. The offense of counseling is its subtly becoming an end in itself instead of one of many instruments used by the Holy Spirit to shepherd God's people. Confession to a friend, the Easter morning liturgy, a familiar assurance of pardon, a lighted candle, a week building an adobe church in New Mexico, can become pastoral activities.

Implications for Pastoral Preaching

A rhythm "of a positive pattern of action meeting need" and withdrawal is equally important in pastoral preaching.

The Biblical Image of Shepherd

Many of us have experienced a very negative judgmental style of preaching. This kind of preaching goes beyond the categories of "liberal" and "conservative." For whether the topic is "witnessing for Jesus," the necessity of an early morning "quiet time," or the need to take action against nuclear energy, multinational corporations or apartheid, it can be preached in such a way that *the* message is we do not measure up. This message is not counterpoint to the notes of grace—not measuring up is *the* point. So in reaction to that style of preaching, when given the opportunity, we want to proclaim the love of God and the freedom for growth and fulfillment that are ours in Christ. Furthermore, we want our sermons to be of practical help for people who are buffeted about by the swirling winds of social and emotional change. It is no surprise then that "preaching as personal counseling" or "life-situation preaching" appears to be a "positive pattern of action meeting need." The published sermons of Harry Emerson Fosdick and the anthologies of sermons edited by Charles F. Kemp give abundant evidence that this positive, problem-oriented approach can be pastoral. Closer to home, we have observed how people come alive to sermons that address gnawing personal need.

The first church I served had shown a genuine interest in and positive response to the preaching of my predecessor. It was obvious that the sermons preached came right from the "life situations" of the people. This experience made the same people initially wary of my style of preaching. They could not believe that following a plan of Bible lessons over a three-year period could be responsive to the Holy Spirit and the pressing needs of individuals. It was inconceivable that such an organized and balanced series of scripture lessons (the three-year lectionary) could produce "pastoral preaching." At first I downplayed the fact that I was following the lectionary. Despite my commitment to wrestle with the text first many parishioners became convinced that each sermon was a direct response to some incident that had occurred during the week. By the time I moved to another parish I was committed to a plan of speaking over time from the fullness of the biblical witness.

This has meant going beyond problem-centered or need-oriented sermons. To begin with a human need and then apply the wisdom of the Christian scriptures to that need is indeed a form of pastoral action. But it has its serious limitations. What seems an inexhaustible supply of common human problems can easily take on a "this is clearly the problem, this is the positive solution" cadence. Is the personal problem orientation getting at the needs of all the people? Aren't there times when we need to *withdraw* from such direct "problem-centered" preaching?

Pastoral preaching comes from the "whole counsel of God" (not a few "positive" texts) and the fullness of the church year. There are times when the emphasis should fall on what David Babin calls "celebrating health." Liturgical preaching based on the lectionary frees us from beginning always with a crushing human need. Do we always begin there as we come to worship? Indeed the sermon may be a response to the parable of the prodigal father which helps us begin with the outgoing action of a parent's love and the celebration of the ensuing salvation. We need not always begin in the "far country." Babin also reminds us that some of the direct pattern of pastoral action may take place in other parts of the liturgy. Although my study centers on pastoral preaching and not on the pastoral power of worship, in general the two cannot be separated.[8] For instance, when the sermon picks up the gospel response to loneliness or guilt, or grief, the other elements of worship may be meeting our secret longings for praise, confession, forgiveness.

There will be many times when the other movements of the liturgy are much more involved in direct pastoral action. The richness of Christian worship is denied when we try to minister pastorally to one another solely through the sermon. At times we will be compelled by the Holy Spirit to preach a word that is more prophetic than pastoral, or that deals more with social responsibility than personal problems. The preacher needn't think that he or she at that moment ceases to be "an undershepherd of Christ." For if direct pastoral action seems to be withdrawn, it is still present in a liturgy that, again by the power of the Spirit, can speak to individual grief and crisis and call us to social responsibility.

Moreover, neither in the Word read, preached, or enacted is there as clear a border between the prophetic and pastoral as we often assume. Is it not possible for the man or woman who is primarily called to the parish ministry and the care of souls to be a prophet as well? Now by prophet we mean one who has a word from the Lord and proclaims it even when this word judges the status quo or accepted practices of church and society. This word often sets the speaker at odds with powerful forces in and outside the church which seek to defeat God's justice and mercy. A prophet then is more than one who proclaims the Word of the Lord, he or she is one whose life (and life-style) is put on the line by that Word. The prophet is not just another term for political activist or a social visionary. In the biblical tradition the prophet is one who speaks for the Lord. The secular humanist knows the volcanic situation created by one country having 5.8 percent of the world's population and 35 percent of the world's resources. What the secularist doubts is that there is an authentic, applicable word from the Lord. On the other hand some American Christians have a great appetite for "prophetic" visions of the last days and a chronological scenario of the Second Coming. This is not often accompanied by a desire to know what God is saying about austerity, sacrifice, and economic justice.

Perhaps a fundamental weakness within Christianity is our insistence on separating completely the role of the pastor and prophet. In the late 1960s and early 1970s some Christians saw the need for bold prophetic action that would call into question the church's allegiance to cultural values over biblical values. One example of this was Jim Wallis and the Sojourners Fellowship. An *A.D.* magazine article suggests that ". . . the Sojourners Fellowship has matured into what many consider the freshest prophetic voice in American religious life." The group marked from its founding more than a decade ago by "righteous zeal and moral indignation" has recently combined this zeal with an intentional pastoral concern. Wallis is quoted as saying:

> Our greatest struggle is to find a unity between the pastoral and the prophetic. . . . I am not satisfied being a hit-and-run prophet. That leaves a sting of hurt and guilt behind. We have to take more concern if we are going to rebuild the church. It is a pastoral rather than prophetic task.[9]

That statement is highly significant. Many of those who are called to specialized ministries that are engaged in a bold prophetic witness are discovering the necessity of a caring pastoral element in their witness. Likewise those of us who are called to a parish ministry are discovering a prophetic word within the pastoral. We do not have to turn our backs on the pastoral calling and gifts to be a roving prophet speaking truth in the courts of power. In an address entitled "Speaking the Truth to Power," William Sloan Coffin remarked that a judgment on the rich and powerful is rightly seen as mercy for the poor and powerless. Yet he insists that judgment on the rich and powerful also means mercy for the rich and powerful.[10]

I interpret this as meaning the word of judgment to those of us who "have" at the expense of "have nots" is a pastoral, a shepherding word. The pastor who visits the sick and lonely, counsels people in painful circumstances, is asked to preach to these same people a "word of comfort." However within this very pastoral context the prophetic note must be sounded not only for the physical sake of the dispossessed but also for the spiritual sake of the "possessed." If our concern is the "care of souls" can we ignore the bitter enemy of the soul, a desire for more and better that ignores the plight of the poor? The Bible gives ample testimony that judgment on our greed is meant as a sign of spiritual grace for "haves" and "have nots" alike. Spiritual blessing comes to those who give of what they hold as God's stewards to the aliens, orphans, and widows (Deut. 14:28-29).

This idea of judgment as a part of God's grace brings us back to an important aspect of the biblical shepherding perspective. David Alden Steere reminds us that, "Demand and judgment are again timed in order to permit the recipient to undertake greater responsibilities."[11] Greater responsibility means taking a fuller, healthier share in a pastoral community.

We must go beyond the idea of shepherding as the responsibility of the pastoral office and move to an understanding of a "pastoral community." The New Testament idea of spiritual gifts given to *all* Christians, and Luther's "priesthood of all believers" must extend our concept of pastoral care. When Luther first publicly expressed his conviction on the universal priesthood he was giving back to the church its vocation of being priests to one another.[12] Certainly the pastoral office should reflect the "tender solicitous concern" of God for his people. But just as the preacher cannot do all the proclaiming of the gospel, so too the overall ministry of shepherding cannot be left to the ordained pastor. This means that shepherding in all of its manifestations—counsel, discipline, encouragement—can at different times and places be the work of the laity. It has been my experience that with proper training and the utilization of God-given spiritual gifts some of the best "pastoral" preaching and counseling can come from laypeople. This should not be surprising, but a pastoral community does not come into being automatically. The pastoral minister serves as model as well as "enabler" of this shepherding community:

> In the office of the ordained ministry a relationship between pastor and people is established, a pastoral leadership wherein several dimensions of the proclamation of the gospel are integrated: its verbal representation in acts such as preaching, its

27

sacramental presentation in baptism and eucharist, and its personal and societal expressions in caring service. Accordingly pastoral care is not dedicated exclusively to ordained ministers but pastors are responsible for "pastoral oversight."[13]

Vulnerability and Authority

Since the pastor is to be a model it is essential that his or her model is the "great shepherd of the sheep" (Heb. 15:20). As we reflect Jesus' pastoral spirit, the elements of compassion, teaching, discipline, and sacrifice will be in evidence. If the pastor and the pastoring community are to live out the life of the Good Shepherd there must also be in our shepherding vulnerability. He is the one who sends us out "as sheep in the midst of wolves" (Matt. 10:16). Christian shepherds, as Hiltner points out, "Need to utilize any knowledge and wisdom we can get from any source for pastoral care."[14] In other words going out like sheep does not preclude being "wise as serpents." What it does mean is that if our model is really the biblical concept of shepherding we are not allowed to avoid or deny the pain and suffering of this world. Rudolph Bohren has pinpointed the hidden infection that disables our pastoral care. ". . . *it would like to bless without accepting the curse.*"[15]

Indeed one of the criticisms of the shepherding model is its paternalistic nature. It can, and indeed has been used to enforce a rigid separation between "shepherd and sheep." Some of the religious sects have made this distinction a cardinal doctrine. The principle of authority has been emphasized, and consequently almost unquestioned and unlimited power can be placed in the hand of the leaders (shepherds) "for the good of the sheep." This, to me, is evidence of the "hidden infection" that Bohren speaks about. He would argue that our pastoral care requires a fuller understanding of the shepherding metaphor. Bohren sees the midpoint of pastoral care as God who becomes vulnerable. "He places himself in the position of one who needs pastoral care." The great Shepherd of the sheep is also the *Lamb of God* who cries out for help, for care. Then the question comes to us, "Can we exercise pastoral care without ourselves being in need of care?"[16]

In other words, does pastoral authority come from communicating an unassailable bastion of strength in counseling, preaching, and working with the official church boards? The theme of vulnerability will be applied more specifically to sermon development and delivery later. The point here is that alongside all those we minister to we stand in need of God's pastoral care. That care, often mediated through others in the pastoral community, is thwarted when we see ourselves primarily as dispensers of "the blessing." If the shepherding ministry is nothing less than the ministry of the Shepherd God through the body of Christ on earth, then vulnerability cannot be escaped.

Certainly there are pitfalls to a style that confesses doubts, failures, weaknesses. It can become confessional without true repentance and change. If put on from the outside it will last as long as "vulnerability" is in vogue. More than a psychological fad or a communication tool, it must be a part of our growing identity in Christ. If seen as an authentic response to the Shepherd/Lamb the effect on pastoral ministry within the church will be significant. Such a life-style gives others permission to admit their own weaknesses. Also a ministry that does not stand above, but *with* others breaks down artificial and unbiblical distinctions between clergy and laity. There is a difference in office but not in status. That is espoused in almost all Christian denominations. When, however, it is truly lived and practiced we have the beginning of a pastoral community.

In that classic work *The Reformed Pastor,* Richard Baxter says to his fellow pastors, "We have the same sins to mortify and destroy, and we have the same graces to be quickened and strengthened as our people have."[17] The goal of admitting our frailty is never to glorify human weakness. Rather pastoral ministry in and through our humanity is aimed at "that which is the ultimate end of our entire life, even pleasing and glorifying God."[18] This timely reminder by the venerable Puritan pastor of Kidderminster can save us from viewing vulnerability as an ultimate goal.

What may also keep us from a shallow vision of vulnerability is remembering that the word means "unprotected from danger." This definition makes us once again aware of "being sent out as sheep in the midst of wolves." This is the side of pastoral vulnerability we would frequently like to forget. Yet this "nakedness to injury" is a distinguishing characteristic of shepherding. The third element of Steere's biblical model of shepherding, "a sacrificial expenditure of life" cannot be denied. We instinctively (self-preservation) stop short of taking a position or befriending a person that could cause à loss of income or standing. That for most of us is what "sacrificial expenditure of life" can mean. It is not usually physical death, but how much more sensitive are we in this day to a threat to our economic life? Tight job market, inflation, family pressures—how easy it is to sound open and vulnerable in the pulpit but cautiously stay away from any position or person who may cost us a loss. This is not to suggest self-flagellation or reckless behavior in the name of shepherding. Nonetheless, if we are always "playing it safe" when we preach, participate in something, or defend someone, we lose the soul of pastoral care.

On the other hand, if the pastor portrays a "sacrificial expenditure of life," the authority of undershepherd is present and recognizable. Most pastors today have experienced to some degree the professional identity crisis that causes one to question the authority of the church and its ministry. Much has been written about the need for credentialing, accountability, and professional competence. It is not my purpose to recount here the argument for developing and maintaining a professional identity as minister. Rather I wish to raise the question of where our authority comes from:

> Is our authority in the ministry basically justified by our professional competence in certain arts or sciences? . . . The inclusive concept must be pastoral and not professional, a constant concern for the spiritual growth of every member, a reflection of and an exposition on the Great Shepherd who gave his life for the sheep.[19]

Professor Paul, a student of the history of Christian ministry, has correctly pointed to one essential pillar of pastoral authority and authenticity. Professional competence is certainly to be valued. Infinitely more important, however, is the spiritual quality of care and concern expressed in counseling, preaching-teaching, and leadership. In fact, such concern is a participation in the continuing ministry of the Great Shepherd. The authority of our ministry must rest on being a "reflection and an *exposition*" of his sacrificial caring translated into ever-changing cultural patterns and social situations.

Several years ago I was on a committee charged with selecting a person to start a pastoral counseling center which would serve our community. In that process one candidate appeared to have excellent training and credentials in psychology and pastoral counseling. One layperson who had a Ph.D. in one of the behavioral sciences asked, "But does he have a pastor's heart?" Sentimentality. Nostalgia. Soft thinking. Perhaps, but I believed we were seeking a man or woman with the spiritual gifts of a Christian shepherd, willing to make sacrifices for those whom she or he was called to minister. Professional competence, counseling and communication skills are certainly important to an effective pastoral ministry. Yet if that ministry is in the name of and through the power of Jesus Christ, then it will be marked (authenticated) by his active compassion. Jesus had compassion on those who were "harrassed and helpless, like sheep without a shepherd" (Matt. 9:36).

Compassion is a primary ingredient in pastoral authority, but that authority is based on more than the crucial tasks of listening, caring, comforting. For out of Jesus' compassion for the shepherdless sheep, he began to *teach* them. In another passage we read: "He entered the synagogue and taught. And they were astonished at his teaching, for he taught them as one who had authority" (Mark 1:21-22).

Whatever the method or mode of pastoral preaching, it is not pastoral unless the preacher sensitively *listens* to the needs, concerns, fears, and hopes of his or her people. Listening also to the best in current thought in the human arts and science is important. This listening, however, is not the final source of our authority. "If there is any stance that has marked the Christian community in recent years it is that of listening. . . . More specifically it has involved listening to an entity known as 'modern man,' in the expectation that thence will come the redemptive word."[20] If we are to shepherd God's people, we will have to proclaim as well as to listen, doctrine along with dialogue. The truth comes not primarily from listening to modern authorities. The truth is in the Good Shepherd at once *compassionate servant* and *confident teacher-proclaimer.* "Whatever ministry or authority is exercised in his name is derivative and imitative."[21] He is the model *and* source for all pastoral speaking and listening.

At times having been moved by the deepest needs of ourselves and our people, we are then able to listen for an authoritative word that "speaks to our condition." At other times the process may appear to be an authentic word from the Lord that has suddenly broken into what had seemed to be a most mechanical, fruitless "listening" in prayer and study. That word becomes "a fire shut up in my bones" which must be released. It is addressed not only to the pastor but also to the community. Delivering that word is nothing less than a pastoral task.

In the traditional modes of pastoral care[22] authority comes through the quality of Christ-like caring *and* a living Word that mediates God's healing, guiding, sustaining, and reconciling activity in our lives. *Healing* is helping a person who is hurting be restored to a condition of wholeness. One can see how this function of pastoral care has in modern times been related to the insights of depth and humanistic psychologies. Yet the ground for our healing ministry is ultimately in the saving work of Jesus who laid down his life for the sheep (John 10:11). *Guiding* consists of helping people make choices based not only on the temporal but also in "light of eternity." This description pushes us back to its biblical base in the Hebrew word for shepherd, *raah*. As previously stated, this word underscores the importance of strong teaching and nurturing in the pastoral ministry. *Sustaining* implies that full restoration is not immediate or necessarily a possible goal. The emphasis in times of grief, separation, and loss is on enabling the person to endure and transcend his or her circumstances. *Reconciling* means reestablishing broken relationships with God, self, and others. This mode of care speaks to the inner reaches of the fragmented self and to the political and social barriers that are often demonic instruments of separation. The ministry of reconciliation, like the ministry of healing, is rooted in nothing less than the cross of Christ which ultimately conquers all division and hostility (Eph. 2:14-16).

Pastoral Guardianship

Even from this brief summary one can see the biblical-theological roots of each of these traditional modes of pastoral care. Through the ages these four modes have certainly been shaped by and understood through the prevailing social, cultural, and psychological influences of the day. Nonetheless each of these modes can be seen as flowing from the Judeo-Christian image of the Shepherd God. If preaching can be said to be "pastoral" then it will reflect the healing, guiding, sustaining, reconciling activity of God. This list is in no way exhaustive. For example, we have previously made a case for discipline or judgment as a pastoral activity. Whether it is seen as a separate category or is fitted under one of the traditional modes is an open question.

Charles Jefferson in his classic work on the pastor-preacher, *The Minister as Shepherd,* summarized the modes of shepherding as he saw them at work in the great Shepherd of the sheep, Jesus of Nazareth: "I am the Good Pastor," he says, "I *watch,* I *guard,* I *guide,* I *heal,* I *rescue,* I *feed,* I *love* from the beginning, and love to the end. Follow me!"[23] This list touches on basically the same aspects of shepherding as Clebsch and Jaekle's modes, and David Steere's "essential elements" discussed earlier. Yet risking some duplication I would turn the reader's attention to the ministry of pastoral guardianship. Jefferson states emphatically, "We have spent too much time in coaxing half-dead sheep back to life again, and not enough in building barriers against the wolves."[24] Any pastor will quickly recognize the wisdom in Dr. Jefferson's statement. As the health care professionals are beginning to emphasize preventive medicine, marriage and family counselors see the importance of marriage enrichment programs, so pastors must begin to recognize the need for safeguards before a flock of God is divided and driven off. It must be admitted that Jefferson's colorful description of the ministry of guardianship is more suggestive than descriptive. He does not spell out who the wolves are, or what barriers must be erected. However, it is clear that this "work of prevention" he refers to is seen primarily in *moral* categories.[25]

It cannot be denied that we have been turned off by moralistic preaching and afraid of value judgments in counseling. We have consequently not seen the place of Christian values and moral principles in pastoral ministry. Because pastors have not wanted to appear judgmental or legalistic, a primary aspect of pastoral care to troubled and confused individuals has been neglected. The implication is that sensitive preaching and counseling cannot touch on moral issues without becoming moralistic. Perhaps we are now beginning to see that pastoral care must meet the fundamental need "for a structure, a character, an identity, a religiocultural values system out of which to live."[26] We can agree with the concensus that pastoral preaching is preaching to people's needs. Now we must go beyond much of that literature and insist that "people's needs" include the need of a moral-ethical framework in which to make responsible decisions. Our response to legalism need not be the excesses of antinomianism that Paul encountered in the Corinthian church.

Are there not moral-ethical guidelines from the Scriptures which may serve a guardian function in the community of faith? This *is* an important pastoral ministry for the Christian shepherd. She or he who preaches must also be seeking to live under the law of Christ. This law of Christ will always be characterized by the grace to forgive ourselves and others when love is transgressed. Yet forgiveness will never be seen as "it doesn't matter anyway." A sense of God's costly forgiveness will allow us to seek once again the standards of a "city that has foundations." This will mean that the pastoral guardian will be compelled at times to expose those standards and values of this "present age" as a warped reflection of that which endures.

There is another equally valid function of pastoral guardianship that Jefferson did not address in 1912. Nonetheless it has always been a part of the pastoral office. Recently Thomas C. Oden called for a return to "the craft of pastoral guardianship." Dr. Oden reminds us that the office of ministry has been charged with the guardianship of an authentic apostolic witness since its inception and that this guardianship is a pastoral task which falls "mainly on the working pastor."[27] The layperson assumes that the pastor is able to deliver teaching based on "ancient ecumenical Christianity" and be able also to distinguish this doctrine from spurious alternatives.[28] The pastor, according to Oden, does not get much help from the academic theologian in this area of determining sound doctrine. This argument offends our modern sensibilities. We envision Salem witch hunts, or people being read out of a church for a "faulty view" of the atonement. Will pastoral guardianship lead to oppressive, doctrinaire teaching and preaching? No doubt we must hear what Oden is saying with a discerning ear but what he says has a ring of truth to it. We are often so open-minded that we see little place for boundaries in the field of Christian doctrine. Allow as we must for freedom of conscience, and diversity within the Christian community, let us begin to confront heretical teachings that scatter the sheep.

This is not an imaginary or trivial problem. As a pastor I am called on to deal with individual hurt, and church schism that appears in the wake of what must be called false doctrine. We become a people unable to deal with our own humanity (sexuality, health, and sickness) when we allow a suble Doceticism to surface in our understanding of Christ and his church. In other circumstances, Jesus of Nazareth as ethical example, model for humanity, "man for others" is kept neatly away from any embarrassing claims of divinity in fine Ebionite fashion. The excessive example of leaving it to the Spirit at the expense of a fuller Trinitarian view of God may mark us as latter-day Montanists. This does not mean that the modern pastor should decide that the evangelicals or the liberals or the conservatives should be expelled from the true church. What is being said is that teaching which sets up false expectation (i.e., faith will bring material prosperity) should be countered with the depth of the whole counsel of God. The pastor must recover his or her calling as theologian and exercise guardianship by strong doctrinal teaching, preaching, "pastoral admonition and confidential spiritual counsel."[29]

The undershepherd as guardian is a calling fraught with danger (as are all modes of pastoral care). The pastor can become authoritarian, rigid, insensitive, and reactionary. Yet I believe Browning calls for a recovery of the moral context and Oden of the doctrinal context of pastoral care because our age has seen more error in the opposite direction. In the main line churches the virtues of being "open," "non-judgmental," "inclusive," have set the tone for our pastoral speaking and acting. The voices of Oden and Browning are not calling for moralistic and rigid orthodoxy in the pulpit and counseling room. They are part of a corrective, irenic spirit that calls us back to a fuller understanding of pastoral care. This fuller, deeper understanding is reflected in a sermon by Saint Augustine:

> Disturbers are to be rebuked, the low-spirited to be encouraged, the infirm to be supported, objectors confronted, the treacherous guarded against, the unskilled taught, the lazy aroused, the contentious restrained, the haughty repressed, litigants pacified, the poor relieved, the oppressed liberated, the good approved, the evil borne with, and all to be loved (*Sermo* CCIX).[30]

Summary and Definition

Revealed in this sentence from a sermon is the shepherding perspective which should be seen in every truly pastoral sermon. For here is the Good Shepherd's ministry carried on. It was his compassion for the shepherdless and hungry sheep that moved him to teach and feed them. Speaking the truth and speaking it in love cannot be separated. *Pastoral preaching will be marked by a shepherd's compassion and concern which desires nothing less for Christ's flock than the whole counsel of God.*

CHAPTER III

Telling the Whole Truth

There is only one thing in the pulpit more important than telling the truth and that is telling the whole truth. Though it may be added by way of caution that we all have not one Sunday but quite a few in which to do it.[1]

Dr. Scherer's stress on telling the whole truth falls on the harried preacher's ears as one more drumbeat of judgment. Doesn't the repeated use of the phrase "whole counsel of God" in this book sound more like impossible law than liberating grace? They are harsh words on two counts. First, it is difficult to face our congregations with the demanding task to be *helpful,* and *imaginative;* second, it is difficult to be expected to impart *the truth.*[2]

One of our constant goals in preaching is to be helpful. There is no phrase more encouraging to the pastoral preacher than, "That really helped me." The desire to help those we are charged to feed, guide, and guard is not to be taken lightly. Let us not be apologetic for developing a style of pastoral conversation and preaching that is helpful. David Switzer has gone so far as to suggest that the psychologist Carkhuff's conditions for a helpful relationship can be applied to preaching.[3] This may be useful, but a theological critique of "helpfulness" is also required.

The pastoral sermon must be more than a how-to-do-it

lesson . . . it is imaginative. By that I mean preaching that is more than well-thought-out answers to troubling questions. Urban Holmes reminds us that people, rather than seeking only specific answers, come seeking a picture, an image of the presence of God in Christ. This "seeing" is through the imagination. The preacher who visualizes with the colors of his or her own imagination may speak imaginatively to others. Holmes quotes Goethe as saying, "We live in a rainbow, not a pure white light of truth."[4]

Whether pure white or multicolored we are back to the question of truth. Pastoral preaching should be helpful and imaginative, but *it can be neither unless it is truthful.* This is where we shrink back with a certain kind of humility: "Yes I will be truthful in the sense of intellectual honesty, but I have no delusions of speaking *the truth.*" It does at first blush appear immodest to make such truth claims. But the claims are not for our "best ideas." Our preaching is rooted in something deeper than brilliant flashes of insight. The truth we proclaim is made known in Jesus Christ. In making the Scriptures that bear witness to him the anchor of our preaching, we offer "help" that goes leagues beyond our best advice. Commenting on Acts 20:27, John Calvin says, "The whole counsel of God is included in His Word and must not be sought anywhere else." Indeed if our preaching is to be immediately and eternally helpful, we are "to expound scripture faithfully and from it establish the people in faith, in the fear of the Lord, and in all godly practices."[5] *These are pastoral concerns and they are met when our preaching is fully biblical.* For it is in the Bible that the One who claimed to be *the truth* is revealed. This is the necessary starting point for telling the whole truth.

Biblical Preaching as Pastoral Preaching

The practical import of a starting place is not lost on the pastor-preacher: "Do I begin by trying to find some burning issue, or crucial question that arises from human need? Or do I begin with the 'unsearchable riches of Christ' (Eph. 3:8) as it is made known to us in the scripture?" In many ways this old question of whether we should begin in Nashville and move to Jerusalem or vice versa is unanswerable. The question may be, Where do I begin a sermon, with a concrete example of present need, or a retelling of a biblical passage? It is my intention to demonstrate later that a pastoral sermon can begin either place, as long as it is not content to stay there. If, however, our question is really asking what is our *priority* I must come down (with a slight "hedge") on the side of beginning with the prayerful study of the Bible. Throughout our study of "shepherding" in the Bible there emerged the shepherd's call to "feed" the flock. In John 21 it is seen clearly as the response of love to the life-giving love of Christ. If John Milton was right, "and the hungry sheep look up and are not fed" perhaps it is because we shepherds have not spent enough time and energy providing the food that supplies the soul's hunger. Biblical preaching is pastoral because it is out of care and concern for the people of God that we share the best we have.

The slight but important hedge is that the biblical preacher who is also a shepherd will "know the sheep by name." Critical yet prayerful exegesis of a text will yield a word with my name on it and names of those to whom I minister. This does not mean reading my agenda, or even the pressing needs of people, into the text. On the other hand true exegesis of a passage is incomplete until the Word which is heard in its literary and historical setting comes to life in our present setting.

Perhaps another way of answering this question of where to begin is to say, "We begin by *listening*":

> The word of the Scriptures is the revelation of God's action not just in the past but also in the present and future. In the last resort all that is needed is listening, that careful listening in

which one's whole being and one's whole world is laid open to what is to be heard, and then the courage and integrity of prophets and apostles, to speak and act in faithfulness in the situations of our own time.[6]

Listening is the continual task of the pastor. It is not passive. Rather listening calls forth all the discipline and creativity one can muster. Admitting the overwhelming odds against listening "in which one's whole being and one's whole world is laid open" brings a fresh realization of my own weakness and God's grace. It is amazing that any listening takes place. How difficult it is for me to release my tight grip on cherished presuppositions, defenses, and actually listen to another person's story. There is the constant temptation to miss what he or she is saying while I am forming my own response or interpretation.

Aren't these the same forces at work when we are unable to hear a fresh and liberating word from a parable of Jesus, or an incident at Mount Horeb? It is not surprising that much so-called biblical preaching "takes off" from a certain phrase and never returns to the Bible or to the text. As in interpersonal conversation we are not so much engaged in listening as "responding." In speaking of the Bible and pastoral care David Switzer employs one of my favorite phrases from the work of Theodore Reik, "listening with the third ear." "This expression refers to a quality of listening and observing a person which considers the whole human being. It is the attempt to receive the *whole* message not just the literal meaning of the words which the person uses."[7]

Those words, used here to describe listening to a person, could be used to describe listening to the scriptures. Indeed one of the more solid and helpful books on biblical preaching I have read recently applies similar language to exegesis. The book is *The Bible in the Pulpit,* written by New Testament scholar Leander Keck. Keck suggests an intriguing analogy in his discussion of pastoral prayer. A truly *pastoral* prayer implies a relationship with the congregation. It is not prayer about people, or at them, but on their behalf.

> To pray on their behalf, one must enter into their lives to the point that one begins to feel what they feel, yet without losing one's identity as a pastor. What is in view here is a solidarity that does not obscure one's role and office, nor obliterate the capacity for critical judgment and distance. . . .
>
> Listening to the text is an analogous priestly act or process. Priestly listening means listening/hearing in solidarity with the people, vicariously; it is doing so on behalf of the congregation.[8]

Although Dr. Keck speaks of the priestly acts of prayer and "listening to the text" his analogy is suggestive for pastoral counseling and preaching. The pastor attempts to empathize with the individual, "to sit where he or she sits." Yet my experience tells me that "empathetic understanding" is not a given. Listening is a very intentional activity. I find myself continually fighting through my initial impressions and cherished assumptions. Even when some generative level of empathy is achieved one must fight against losing one's personal and pastoral identity. There is a certain "distance" (not to imply aloofness or invulnerability) which is maintained so the counselor is not totally absorbed into the needs-demands of the other. The critical faculties of discernment and judgment must be present in every pastoral relationship.

This style of listening as it is developed in pastoral counseling has a concomitant value which is not always recognized. I worked in counseling for several years before preaching became a part of my ministry. Now I realize my counseling had involved exegesis that was not unlike the exegesis required for hearing a passage of scripture. A counselor's empathetic listening cannot be separated from the task of asking the right questions and exercising critical judgment. The pastor who works hard at allowing the person to speak for himself or herself works just as hard at allowing the text to speak for itself. Just as the pastoral counselor never ceases to represent and listen on behalf of the whole church, the same can be said of the biblical exegete. The church's *pastoral* ministry is reflected in both.

We do well to remember that a distinctive mark of shepherding (or pastoring) is "a sacrificial expenditure of life." We have often heard this as a romantic ideal unrelated to the daily work of the pastor. However, it is this facet of the shepherding perspective that must be applied to the common, yet crucial, task of listening. The bane of pastoral ministry is, to use a phrase made popular by radio, "easy listening." It is my temptation to hear what I want to hear and to stop listening when I have the answer or the *obvious* sermon topic. Pastoral listening is always costly and demands an expenditure of time, energy . . . life. The cost tells a great deal about the importance of the task.

Perhaps this costliness also tells us why American preaching has placed so little emphasis on biblical exegesis. Dr. David H. C. Read, in describing some renewed interest in biblical (even lectionary) preaching, noted that this is not an American tradition.[9] He observed that many seminaries do an adequate job of emphasizing sound exegesis; the wrestling with the then and now of the text. Yet something happens between classroom and pulpit. Many American preachers fall into a topical, "relevant" approach which often sacrifices the power that comes from living with a passage of scripture. That Read had "ears to hear" American preaching was evident when he listed the two main reasons pastors settle for something less than biblical preaching. One is the sheer mechanics of running a church, which pushes against the firm resolve to spend the hours necessary for grappling with a biblical text. Second, he described what happens when we don't spend time on exegesis, or preparing the exposition, and the sermon is well received. This positive evaluation becomes an excuse for shortcuts the next time around. Soon a pattern is developed.

Dr. Read's analysis is painfully correct. In response I can

offer no protection from administrative pressures, or the lure of prepackaged sermon "aids." However my own experience of meeting weekly with one or more other ministers for a few hours to work on the lectionary lessons for the coming Sunday provides a needed stimulus for biblical-pastoral preaching. This does much to keep us alive to the manifold riches to be found in the Bible. Add some interested laypeople to the group and the possibility of "listening on behalf of the people" is increased.

The emphasis in this discussion of "biblical preaching as pastoral preaching" has been unapologetically on *listening*. Listening is the link that connects the several modes of pastoral ministry. Yet this critical sensitive listening should never be understood as terminal, or even passive. We listen so that we might hear the cry of our common humanity and the life changing Word of God. Having heard, the Word is preached even (or especially) when it judges our pretentions, the church's coldness, or the culture's dearest assumptions. One could dare face such obstacles only if armed with the truth. The saving grace of Dr. Scherer's stress on telling the whole truth is that we do not have to produce that truth. Therefore we need not be diffident about the truth we proclaim. Ultimately it is born not of our best insights and diligent research, but comes to us as a gift in the Christ of the Scriptures.

The Lectionary: A Shepherd's Plan

In the beginning of this chapter I stated that Dr. Scherer's summons to tell the whole truth sounded harsh on two counts. Not only does it appear on the surface to be presumptuous or absurd to claim to speak *the* truth, but also it is difficult to live up to the demand of preaching the *whole* truth. No preacher can proclaim all that is revealed in the Scripture. Theologian Carl Braaten is quite right when he suggests that even for Paul preaching the "whole counsel of God" was an eschatological notion. "After all it was he who said that now our knowledge is partial but in the end it will be whole (I Corinthians 13:12)." Yet we are committed to the vision of the whole . . . our hope and our goal.[10] This goal and hope calls us beyond our own truncated versions of the gospel to an ever fuller understanding of God in Christ. There is always more truth to learn, experience, and preach.

Fortunately, *all* of it doesn't have to be preached this Sunday. That the pastor who preaches has more than one Sunday to proclaim the whole truth may appear to be an obvious or even ridiculous reminder. In reality it is an unexpected note of grace for the woman or man in the pulpit who subconsciously is obsessed with "getting it all said." No matter the text or sermon topic, there is a subtle pressure on even experienced preachers to "cover all the bases" *this Sunday*. I am convinced that a plan of preaching based on the lectionary serves as reminder and demonstration of the shepherding perspective. *The shepherd's relationship to the flock is one of care and concern demonstrated over time.* The Christian pastor is not a guest speaker or visiting evangelist. He or she is able to view the spiritual needs of the congregation and the unfolding drama of the Bible with a wider angle of vision than is provided by one Sunday's agenda. If the shepherd's "longer view" is absent we do violence to the sermon by requiring it to carry a heavier load than it can bear.

An example of this is the temptation to tack on a mini-message on evangelism or world hunger even though it doesn't fit the biblical or pastoral setting of the sermon. In preaching from the Book of James last year I had to continually resist the urge to give equal time in the sermon to the doctrine of justification by faith. However, in living for a while with the lectionary a trust in the wholeness of the biblical witness evolves. You do not find yourself in a such a hurry to do a "balancing act" within each sermon. The faith-in-action message of James is given greater power when the preacher is assured that there will be other Sundays when the corresponding truth of *sola fides* may be accentuated.

Here we should be reminded again that the theological balance we seek comes through the variety *within* the morning liturgy (see p. 24) and the successive emphases of the church year. The word successive is used because I believe, especially in the Gospel lessons, there is a sense of movement from Advent to Pentecost or Kingdomtide. The sense of dramatic movement comes from being caught up in the progressive recitation of the mighty acts of God in Christ. By ordering our worship and preaching around the successive emphases of the Christian Year, a type of pastoral guardianship is practiced.

Growing out of our study of the biblical image of shepherd is the picture of one who guards the flock of God from false or shallow teaching. This can take the form of an unhealthy stress on one or two doctrines with the veritable exclusion of others. Let me give but one composite example of this: a weekly study group may be formed during the season of Pentecost in response to a series of sermons and readings on the Holy Spirit. People in the group express their need to understand and experience the work of the Holy Spirit. The absence of teaching and preaching on the Holy Spirit has left some of them with confusion, apathy, suspicion. On the other hand ecstasy without substance, power without love, marks the experience of others. Worship and study based on the lectionary helps us guard against such dangerous omissions.

The shepherd who is called to guardianship is also given the task of nourishing the flock through the living Word of God. The two are closely related. Before one can talk about a balanced plan of spiritual nourishment for a growing congregation there is a need to guard against our penchant for plunging after the "food" that seems to be swimming closest to the surface. Phillips Brooks' image of the gulls foraging for food is all too clear:

All the vast range of God's revelation and of man's duty is open to you. And how do you proceed? You float over the whole sea of truth, and plunge here and there, like a gull, on every subject that either suits your mood, or that some casual and superficial intercourse with people makes you conceive to be required by a popular need.[11]

This sea-gull method of sermon preparation can lead to pretty skimpy fare for pastor and congregation alike. Even with diligent, prayerful study one can easily fall prey to an overemphasis on one issue, one doctrine, even one book of the Bible. Preaching from the lectionary assists the pastoral preacher to combat these tendencies. Over the course of a year you will discover the rich diversity of biblical and theological themes that are related to the needs of individuals and society.

The last assertion may be the most difficult to accept. A preacher may indeed be convinced that preaching from the lectionary will aid in developing more theological balance and biblical depth. Yet it is quite another matter to convince him or her that it is a helpful tool in speaking to pressing social and personal need. The most frequently heard criticism of lectionary or liturgical preaching is that it is too confining. There is a fear that in mindlessly following a set plan of Bible lessons we will fall into a style of preaching that tells us much about the "ancient Jebusites" but little about ourselves. This type of biblical preaching drove Harry Emerson Fosdick to look for a new way of preaching to people's needs.

To start with a passage from Moses, Jeremiah, Paul or John and spend the first half of the sermon or more on its historic explanation and exposition presupposed the assumption that the congregation came to church that morning primarily concerned about the meaning of those ancient texts.[12]

If this so-called expository preaching gave only a flat historical explanation not many listeners could be expected to come back for the continuation of the story. Following the lectionary with this style of preaching would only prolong the listener's boredom. But the fault is not in the Bible or a plan of preaching from biblical lessons. For true biblical preaching is just the opposite of *mindlessly* following a set plan. As I am listening and asking questions of myself, of the people I minister to, and of the society I live in, my mind is more alive to the voice of God in the secular settings of the Bible. Likewise as I wrestle with biblical texts encountered in the lectionary week after week I am astounded at how they seem to open up and shed light on the most vexing personal and social problems. The texts must be heard by one who is not isolated from people. The people must be ministered to by one who is unafraid to spend time, week after week, listening to the Bible. If this be the case we can agree with Roger Keller: "In the course of a year far more human joys and sorrows, hopes and fears, problems and situations are dealt with through lectionary preaching than are likely to be addressed by any other method of sermon planning!"[13]

This has been my experience. When I am working on the next week's lectionary readings often a particular passage will "choose me" instead of the other way around. If I had been listening *only* to the voices in recent counseling sessions, periodicals, and pastoral visits, a problem that impacts on all of us may still have been missed. This was the case in a sermon preached recently on the Christian view of the body. The epistle lesson brought alive a biblical view of the physical and the sexual which is far superior to idolatry on the one hand and denial or rejection on the other. Once this affirmation was heard the "text walked around with me" and the need for such a word was apparent in a diversity of pastoral encounters. Conversely I saw the text more clearly as I visualized our ever-present struggles to accept who we are as physical beings of a certain shape, size, and density! The feedback after the sermon convinced me that no sermon could be more "topical." Yet hopefully that is because it was true to the biblical text, the larger context of scripture, and the life situations of its hearers.

The experience of being chosen by a text brings to mind the vast amount of homiletical literature on how to choose a subject for preaching. This literature grows out of a historic emphasis on the personal prerogatives of the preacher. The American Free Church tradition has been especially leary of any infringement on the right of pastors to choose, develop, and deliver their own material. Hence the history of the American pulpit reveals a high regard for the independent, virtuoso performance. True, we no longer live in the era of the pulpit giants. However our worship is still preacher-centered in that other portions of the liturgy are seen as preliminaries or backdrops for preaching. Liturgy is not actually experienced as "the work of the people." Furthermore we can be led to believe that the congregation's *only* participation in the sermon event is the grateful response: "Pastor, I don't see how you come up with great ideas Sunday after Sunday."

An alternative to this individualism is suggested in yet another consequence of viewing the lectionary from a shepherding perspective. The lectionary *becomes a practical reminder of the church as pastoral community.* Shepherding is not the work of one person or office (see p. 27). It is ultimately the whole church which lives out the ministry of the Good Shepherd. Ordained ministers are indeed responsible for "pastoral oversight." However the total ministry of the church must go beyond the resources of any one person. This is true in the realm of preaching *in* worship. Liturgy truly becomes "the work of the people" when all the people are contributing their spiritual gifts to the worship of God.

This *laos*, or people of God, is not even confined to those living believers present on a given Sunday morning. The Christian doctrine of "the communion of saints" reminds us that we are members of a continuing tradition that spans the centuries. In making use of the resources of the Christian Year we are utilizing the most powerful thoughts and prayers of all ages. Our words must finally be contemporary. But how much more universal they become when in dialogue with the "works of the teachers and saints of the Christian Church." Charles Williams said that it "sometimes seems a pity that we should prefer the looser and less powerful exhortations of contemporary piety."[14] One of the blessings from the tradition of the church calendar is that it has put me in contact with the pastoral insights of Ambrose, Augustine, John Donne, and many others. These insights coming through the rhythmical pattern of the church year are beneficial in the pastoral task of nurturing people in the faith.

Of course the pastoral community is also made up of those saints who seem much "less" saintly (partly because they are still alive!). This lively fellowship of sinner-saints can keep our sermons from being the work of a solitary scholar. Pastoral counseling, conversation, and visitation brings us close to the life issues confronting individuals and our community. While thinking theologically about the lectionary passages, we are also reflecting theologically on our pastoral encounters. It is in this interface that creative preaching is formed. Previously I mentioned the value of having a study group which includes laypeople to work through the biblical text for that week. This is a way of being more intentional in bringing the text to focus on the needs of people and vice versa.

Recently I have been experimenting with ways in which to extend the lectionary's impact on the congregation. The pastoral value of systematic reading and reflection on the scriptures bids us to go beyond their being read in the Sunday morning service. For the past several years the lectionary lessons for the coming week have been printed in the church bulletin. Those who read the lessons during the week found a balanced foundation for their personal devotions. In addition small groups used these readings (especially during Advent and Lent) as a basis of a disciplined Bible study. There are many ways then that the lectionary can become a means of ministry. The possibilities in our congregation have barely been touched. I am impressed with such devotional commentaries as *The Upper Room Disciplines* which provide an impetus to daily use of the lectionary readings. Also the comments on the scripture readings faithfully challenge us to go beyond "personal devotion" to an acting out of a truly biblical faith.

As the use of the lectionary through the week is increased, there is a heightened sense of preparation for worship. The liturgist and preacher can "feel" the involvement of those already caught up in the drama of the biblical text. If the greater use of the lectionary and the Christian Year increases our involvement in congregational worship, it also draws us closer to the reality of the church universal. The lectionary has provided common ground in ecumenical celebrations of festival days and Sunday liturgies. Furthermore, it is also a small but welcomed reminder of the "tie that binds" our various denominations together. Despite differences of polity, tradition, and doctrinal emphasis we are called to preach the Word of God, in season and out of season.

Some Reservations on the Use of the Lectionary

During the "Fosdick Convocation on Preaching" in October of 1978 Ernest T. Campbell, formerly senior minister of Riverside Church, addressed a group of ministers from around the country on the topic of sermon construction. I remember clearly his insistence that a strong theological foundation must undergird sermon construction and delivery. To use his image, "If the theological and biblical 'spinal column' is wrong all the illustrative material in the world won't save it." It was not surprising that he saw the value of using the lectionary, but he offered this warning:

I must admit to being able to generate two cheers for the lectionary, but not three . . . on the grounds that I'm not always

51

sure the good brothers and sisters who put it together had the advantage of our contemporary exegetical knowledge. In the main it keeps us from riding our hobbies and forces us into areas that we might otherwise not look into.

There are indeed problems with the three-year lectionary now being used by more and more churches. Anyone having used this lectionary can cite examples of texts that are forced into a common theme. Also Brian McCarthy notes that the current lectionary loses many important Old Testament readings by the rule of coordinating the Old Testament reading with the gospel for the day. He suggests a longer cycle of Old Testament readings (five to seven years) to go with a three- or four-year cycle of Gospel and Epistle readings. His suggestions about the Old Testament lessons should be seriously considered, since this is a weakness of the current lectionary. His concluding statement is a helpful guide in approaching the lectionary: "The new lectionary when measured by the norm of the whole Bible is a great step in the right direction, but it is only a first step."[15]

George Sweazey in his excellent text on preaching also airs some reservations about preaching from the lectionary. Some of his objections, however, are already being met by changes in usage of the church calendar. He speaks of no Sunday to mark the "Atoning Work of Christ." Yet many churches that do not have well-attended Good Friday observances are marking a Sunday before Easter as Passion Sunday. Furthermore his objections concerning the proportions of the liturgical year could be resolved by implementing correctives similar to those proposed by McCarthy and others. His suggestion that we miss the spiritual and social needs of our congregation by following the lectionary is not born out by my experience. He gives the illustration of a minister who sees groups in the church gaining an interest in the Holy Spirit; and saying to himself, "I will preach on that next June." First, the season of Pentecost is not the only season which contains passages rich in the theology of the Holy Spirit. Second, any sensitive pastor would not put slavish allegiance to the lectionary ahead of his or her own responsiveness to the clear leading of the Spirit. To choose an alternate text would be far superior to showing ingenuity in "getting from the texts to the sermons they know should be preached."[16]

Before abandoning the texts for a given Sunday, I would read them very carefully. Often a living Word addressed to people caught up in a local or national emergency is found hidden in the lectionary texts. What I am calling for is not an exercise in eisegesis to protect the record of the lectionary. There *will* be times when sermon plans need to be laid aside. The plea here is simply not to turn too hastily from the guidance of the lectionary. Yet, the creative freedom of the Holy Spirit will lead us from time to time to go beyond the ordered lections of the Christian Year. But is it not the same Spirit who most often kindles the pastoral imagination when we look through the disciplined, rooted perspective of the lectionary?

At its best the lectionary remains for pastor and people alike an instrument of guardianship. It can keep us from a *subjectivism* that neglects the need for well-balanced biblical preaching. Such a need is not new or a minor one. The anonymous eighteenth-century work, *A Letter from a Blacksmith to the Ministers and Elders of the Church of Scotland,* contains a fervent plea for pastoral guardianship in the form of a "regular plan of reading" the Scriptures in worship. No clearer warning against the danger of subjectivism in preaching and worship can be issued. Let it be balanced by a warning against an *objectivism* that makes of the lectionary an idol instead of a pastoral staff. If Campbell is correct and we sometimes "hide out in a lectionary against real clamoring need," then it has become a hindrance to the gospel and should be abandoned. The lectionary is not to be canonized. It is not an object to be worshiped, but one pastoral aid to be used in the service of the Good Shepherd.

CHAPTER IV

The Practice of Pastoral Preaching

The high art of walking is one which the minister must master. . . . His usefulness depends upon the evenness and continuousness of his labors. He is a shepherd and shepherds neither fly nor run. A shepherd's work is prosaic, tedious, slow and obscure. Feeding sheep is his daily task.[1]

This statement reflects the soul of the shepherd's perspective, yet how alien it seems to the world of parish ministry in the 1980s. In every phase of pastoral practice we are looking for track shoes, if not wings. Across denominational lines there are strategies for substantial growth (membership) in a one- to three-year period. There is a spate of books available on management by objectives and goal setting applied to the parish (if only we had time to read them). If a pastor is not running ahead of his or her people into the issues that will dominate the twenty-first century, there is a sense of losing ground. While we are frantically trying to keep up, Jefferson's words about sheep and shepherds sound like a bucolic idyll. Nothing could be further from the truth. Charles Jefferson's ministry was in a large parish in New York City, and he was constantly involved in a prophetic ministry addressed to the moral and economic ills of society. Yet he knew where the center of his ministry was. His calling, and daily task, was to feed the sheep.

It is this pastoral perspective when applied to preaching that speaks a word of judgment on our constant search for shortcuts and time-savers. Our craving for quick and easy outlines, sermon starters, and the like betray a concept of ministry dominated by some model other than "shepherd." Those of us who must prepare sermons every week despite full-time "administrative" duties have no interest in that which is "prosaic, tedious, slow, and obscure." But how else can you describe the work of reading, guiding, praying, listening? It is not the place for instant recognition or gratification. Think of the hours of seemingly fruitless wrestling with an unyielding text, the trips to the emergency room, dealing with your own family crises. All of that lies behind the twenty minutes of preaching on Sunday morning.

This description is not meant to be melodramatic or self-serving. For there is gratification; there are compensations. The greatest reward is to know that you have been called into the ministry of the Good Shepherd, who continues to give you the grace to hear his voice in and above the din of all other voices. To see people gradually catch the vision of being a pastoral community meeting human need in and outside the "fold"—that is gratification. None of this is instant. For a part of the pastoral community's meeting need in the name of Christ is accepting the way of "plodders," who seldom run or soar. The One who was moved with compassion when he saw the hungry and the shepherdless must have said and done the same things endlessly. Is there another form of pastoral ministry for those of us who are called to walk with him?

"Indirect Preparation" for Preaching

If the shepherding perspective does represent a commitment to disciplined and continuous ministry over time, then should not this perspective be evident in our approach to sermon preparation? Most pastors have a firmly established approach to weekly sermon construction. What has been slighted or even ignored is the intentional preparation of the minister as pastor and person. Our calling is to the care and feeding of the people of God. However, the Christian shepherd soon learns that the resources needed for an immediate task (i.e., a sermon or a counseling session) come from the daily disciplines of indirect preparation. These disciplines are not directed specifically to preaching, but prepare us to minister in a variety of situations and settings. However, it is not to be doubted that these disciplines have a great deal to do with the quality of pastoral preaching. If we could become as intentional about these disciplines as we are about our methods of weekly sermon preparation the effect would be far-reaching.

A few years ago I found a helpful outline for checking on my own progress in this task of indirect preparation. The outline was found in a most unlikely place—the writings of Sir Francis Bacon. Sir Francis Bacon, as will be remembered, wrote "of many things": "Of Friendship," "Of Gardens," and even "Of Revenge." In his essay "Of Studies" is one sentence that suggests much for the continual task of preparation: "Reading maketh a full man, conference a ready man, and writing an exact man."[2]

Although unintentionally, Bacon does speak to the needs of men and women engaged in pastoral ministry and in "the service of the Word." We rejoice that it is finally the Holy Spirit and not our own effort that gives power to the proclamation of this Word. This does not, however, relieve us from the responsibility of faithful, steady preparation. While preaching is but one facet of the pastoral ministry it will come to reflect the fullness of that ministry.

"Fullness" is exactly what Bacon sees in the discipline of reading. He allows for some reading which has been extracted and distilled by others, but he warns that these "distilled books are like common distilled waters, flashy things." Often these "flashy things" become the core of our reading. The pastor or priest knows all too well the limited amount of time and energy that must be stretched over the broad expanses of the parish round. Therefore, when an opportunity to read appears there is a natural attraction to digests, condensations, and books of "popular theology." The late William Barclay in his autobiography warned, "The most fatal thing of all is to read nothing but other people's sermons . . . and to read nothing but the so-called 'devotional' commentaries."[3]

This is a most arresting statement coming as it does from William Barclay, for his devotional words and popular commentaries continue to be of real help to many pastors. Yet we as pastors in our limited sphere stand in the same position William Barclay did in his "wider" parish. To be a pastor-theologian is to be a "popularizer." By that I mean working our way through the best of theological thought and biblical studies until they can be heard by the nonspecialist. The danger in depending only on predigested works of theology and devotion is that we are allowing someone else to do our intellectual and spiritual grappling.

Admittedly the average pastor cannot read the number of "heavy weights" he or she should. Reasonable reading goals however can be set. This means planning to read a small number of substantial books each quarter for the good of mind and soul. These should include at least one or two commentaries, or biblical studies of the first rank, and a volume of philosophy or theology that presents a challenge to the preacher's thinking. These should be complimented by works of literature, biography, and of the various sciences (including social, political, and such). Of course not every quarter of the year will reflect such depth and variety. My own practice is to keep a list of books read throughout the year. After the end of the year the list is divided into various categories such as those suggested above. This allows me to see over a period of years what are the big gaps in my reading. Again the discipline of reading is not merely preparation for preaching. I find this reading plan to be a factor in my own personal development and a way of expanding my social sensibilities.

At the heart of a pastor's reading discipline is a regular diet of biblical study. My own devotional study centers on working ahead in the lectionary readings for the coming weeks. The emphasis here is listening for the Word of God directed to me; although this does not mean that secondary works are ignored.[4] I take note of any themes that emerge from my readings and usually record these responses in my journal. The second phase of my biblical study has been alluded to in the preceding paragraph. I try to work through one biblical book or a particular area of biblical study (i.e., Old Testament apocalyptic literature, or Paul's use of "in Christ"). This study is helpful in filling in the gaps of the lectionary readings. Working through a book of the Bible or a thematic study invariably takes longer than I had planned. It is an endless round of "picking it up and setting it down again." The truth is often the "setting it down" dominates. My discipline is far from perfect, but I am convinced that these attempts at a regular reading plan can bear much fruit for a fuller life and in fuller preaching.

If we are truly being prepared as pastors and persons the study will not become a cloister, but an entry way into the world of human need and suffering. P. T. Forsyth serves as an example to me of how one can be engaged in regular and thoughtful reading without being cut off from what he described as "the press and care of life." "I was in a relation of life, duty, and responsibility for others. I could not contemplate conclusions without asking how they would affect these people, and my word to them in doubt, death and grief, or repentance."[5] Forsyth's description brings to mind our earlier discussion of pastoral listening. When conversing with the biblical text or a theological treatise the shepherd cannot help seeing the faces of those to whom he or she ministers.

Although it is more common to speak of pastoral counseling, the term "conference" might well be used to refer to the far-reaching person-to-person ministry of the pastor. Without having thought much about the phrase we automatically speak about drop-in and scheduled counseling as "being in conference." The first definition under "con-fer-ence" in *Webster's New World Dictionary* is "conversing or consulting on a serious matter." To a generation of pastors trained in the techniques of counseling and Clinical Pastoral Education, "conversing" may bring up visions of ministerial small talk in the living rooms of the parish. Yet I am convinced that conference or conversation points to a wider, richer field of pastoral practice than does the word "counseling." Pastoral conversation is not bound by the limits of a formal counseling interview. I can remember trying to organize counseling in my first parish on "a counseling center" model. Fortunately it did not take long to discover that a small part of my pastoral care to individuals would take the form of a fifty-minute therapy session.

Indeed, if the pastor is sensitive and prepared to listen and respond, the most superficial conversation may give way to genuine pastoral care. Our conversation can go beyond "individualized preaching" on the one hand, and "non-directive counseling" on the other. Pastoral conversation is marked by empathetic listening to the other person. It is also marked by speech and silence which grows out of our continuous hearing of the Word of God. After hearing the Word of God, we are able to stand *with* a person, identify with his or her joy and pain. As servants of the living Word our conversation is gradually shaped by the presence of the One who has laid down his life for the sheep. The pastor represents and symbolizes the Servant-Shepherd and the community of faith. Perhaps unconsciously this is precisely why a person has sought us out rather than a close friend, psychologist, or social worker. Our conversation is more than two people speaking together. "The pastoral conversation finds its fulfillment there where the Strange Word is heard, where the Third Party enters the conversation."[6] When the Third Party enters the conversation, the pastor is addressed no less than the other person.

That is why conference is such a crucial discipline. As *persons* we are stretched and shaped in new ways when the people we care for gradually (sometimes suddenly) open themselves to us. This happens not only in scheduled sessions in the pastor's study, but in homes, offices, and hospitals. Fortunately the serious matter we are conversing about (Little League baseball, the cost of housing) may be the opening for expressing one's deepest hopes and fears. This discipline is regular, "plodding work." Often the conversation seems to lead nowhere until by "grace-full" serendipity the Third Party slips quietly into our conference. The airport terminal, the hospital corridor becomes an Emmaus Road, in that we are always surprised by the presence of the One who promised to be there.

These encounters with Christ in the needs of our people become great sources of preparation for the preaching event. But we must remember that such preparation for preaching is indirect. The primary reason for entering into a pastoral conference is not to prepare people for our preaching, or to prepare ourselves for preaching. Much less is it to garner sermon illustrations. Rather each conversation is to have the purpose of hearing and responding to another person. But as we hear that person's story it is heard in the context of the gospel story. Likewise when we go again to the pulpit to tell that ancient tale it is as people who have heard it afresh in the Scriptures and in the lives of our brothers and sisters. Coming from the continual discipline of pastoral conversation we are "*ready* at any time to give a quiet and reverent answer to any man who wants a reason for the hope" that is in us (I Pet. 3:15 Phillips, italics mine).

Another form of preparation which is often overlooked is writing. By writing I am not now referring to the writing out of a sermon manuscript or outline. What Bacon refers to when he says it makes one "exact" is the steady *discipline* of writing. Certainly writing is dependent on the two preceding disciplines of reading and conference. Unless a person experiences the fullness of reading and is shaped by his or her relationship with others there will be little to write. Conversely it is writing that enables us to become clearer in thinking and more exact in communication. Often our reading and conversation results in hazy impressions. Perhaps this is because we taste more than we can digest. When, however, I take a few minutes to reshape the content of my reading in my own words, or sketch a "verbatum" of an important conversation, it is amazing how issues and reactions become more distinct. Writing it down appears to be the key.

This exercise for clarifying and retaining is not only for formal study. Elton Trueblood never misses a chance to remind his former students of the value in carrying a small note pad for instant use. He is his own best example. More than once I have seen him pause in a crowded room to jot down some thought or observation that he would not trust to memory. Think now of the flashes of insight, names of people to pray for that have been lost for want of a note pad and the habit of writing in it.

Another small investment of time paying great dividends is the keeping of a journal. It need not be an elaborate undertaking. A page written at the end of a day to crystalize our thinking, feeling, and responding is helpful beyond measure. This single exercise helps us grasp those impressions that have whirled around inside, unnamed, and perhaps even unrecognized. The form and content of my own journal is always changing. During a certain period it will be very introspective; other times it seems to be primarily my reactions to events and ideas. Imperfect though it may be it is a way of listening to my own story. When I am not keeping a journal it is more difficult to be honest with God and with myself. For even in personal meditation there is something about writing out your inner dialogue that increases clarity and understanding.

This movement toward greater exactness is a legitimate goal of writing. The pastor should be engaged in some form of writing every week: church newsletters, book reviews, or a religious column in a local newspaper. Every kind of writing worked at diligently is a preparation for the ongoing task of communication.

These indirect methods of sermon preparation cannot be overemphasized. No plan of sermon construction and delivery can compensate for the lack of continuous preparation done in the context of pastoral ministry. As wide ranging and applicable as this outline derived from Sir Francis Bacon may be, it leaves out the one form of preparation that is the biggest factor in shaping the preacher and the sermon:

> Reading is good, hearing is good, conversation and meditation are good; but then, they are only good at times and occasions, in a certain degree. . . . But the spirit of prayer is for all times and all occasions; it is a lamp that is to be always burning, a light to be ever shining; everything calls for it, everything is to be done in it and governed by it, . . .[7]

William Law's emphasis on prayer for all times and occasions is not another indirect discipline, but the thread that weaves the others together in a pattern of continuous preparation.

In recent works on preaching the place of prayer receives scant attention—perhaps it sounds too pietistic to be "practical." Yet prayer is not the embroidering around the preaching event, but is found in the warp and woof of preaching. Laypeople and ministers may be conscious of this thread of prayer only when it becomes visible in the fabric of worship on Sunday morning. (I am thinking especially here of the "Prayer of Illumination" and "Pastoral Prayer" as they form a part of the liturgy.) But for the "shepherd of souls" the prayer for illumination begins with the inarticulate plea for light and understanding as he or she is engaged in reading the Bible and other literature. When personal and social problems emerge in our pastoral counseling and community involvement, isn't there a prayer for wisdom in the wake of overwhelming complexity? It is this prayer, always in the background, that allows us to go beyond the lure of simple answers.

Theologian Daniel Day Williams has reminded us that one facet of prayer is self-knowledge. He views this "self-knowledge as a dimension of the Christian life and of the pastor's preparation."[8] Indeed the life previously unexamined is deadly in the pulpit. If self-knowledge is neglected the preacher's own needs will dominate the preaching ministry. Therefore writing (such as a journal) which demands searching in the dark corners of mind and will becomes a prayer for illumination *before* the pulpit is ever approached. This thread of prayer can also be seen as our reading, conversation, and writing bring before us those people and situations that call us to prayer of intercession. This process is pastoral prayer. Our public prayers are a small part of the persistent discipline of prayer. All of our preparation for preaching "is to be done in, and governed by it."

From Monday to Sunday

In discussing direct preparation for pastoral preaching two things should be noted. First, the pastor's sermon construction and delivery will be largely a product of the indirect preparation described above. Since this indirect preparation has been neglected in much of the current literature on preaching and because it is vital to the shepherd's work (see p. 56) our emphasis has fallen there. Second, the pattern of direct preparation will vary greatly with the pastor's personality, experience, and the shape of his or her present "charge." All of this leads me to be brief and somewhat sketchy in outlining a week of direct preparation. The outline is not meant to be a step-by-step guide for pastoral preaching. It is a glimpse at one pastor's approach. Now I trust the tone is not too apologetic, because a pastoral theology of preaching cannot be isolated from such a routine chore as sermon construction. It is my hope that the following may lead to creative experimentation in developing pastoral sermons that grow out of a shepherding perspective and one's own unique experience.

On Monday I usually sit down with the lectionary readings and notes taken previously to determine what the primary text will be for Sunday. This is a relaxed rereading of the passages to determine if any or all "hit me" differently now than in my last encounters with them. During the previous season of the church year I will have tentatively mapped out sermon texts and themes for the coming months or season. (This is done by taking some reading days away from the parish and concentrating on this task of sermon planning.) More recently (see p. 58) these passages have formed the basis of my devotional study, and impressions, personal reactions to what I "heard" were jotted down. Unless a pericope has so engaged me that I cannot leave it alone, the work on the primary text is not begun until the next day.

Then Tuesday, or at the latest Wednesday, time is blocked out for digging deeper into the text. Almost all the manuals on preaching advise doing exegetical study in the morning when you are "fresh." No doubt this is sound advice. For me, however, the best rhythm has been morning prayers followed by office work, returning calls, and outlining the rest of the week's schedule with the secretary. Then after lunch I am ready to begin a serious conversation with the text. Since I don't go into the office on Mondays, part of Tuesday morning is needed to clear the deck for serious study. This frees my mind for the major engagement of the day. Yet at the same time the morning activity reminds me that exegesis is not isolated from the "press and care of life."

I try, when possible, to do a part of my study of the text with other people. This is a powerful reminder of the church as a shepherding community. For instance, one summer I participated with a group of high school and college students who attempted to wrestle responsibly with the Epistle readings. Other groups have included ministers, lay leaders, and seminary students. Each group has made its own contribution to sermon preparation, but none can replace a systematic yet flexible approach to exegesis.

Whether I am a part of a group or not, an adequate worksheet is a must. The worksheet is a creative tool in maintaining the balance necessary to preach week to week before the same congregation. The balance I refer to is not theological balance, an impossibility in every sermon. Rather it means that each sermon is to some degree: helpful, truthful, and imaginative. Preaching that focuses exclusively on *helpful* insights for practical living may come from a genuine concern for people, but shallow or superficial biblical study. Being helpful from a biblical viewpoint may well mean a call to repentance and even restitution. Then again preaching may be *truthful* in that it comes from a rigorous conversation with the Scriptures, but this truth may not be translated in terms of the listener's experience. Finally, the preacher may work assiduously on the text keeping the needs of the people in mind, yet fail to preach *imaginatively*. Preaching is not a prosaic lecture. The imaginative literature of the Bible must speak to the imagination of the listener. Not only should the sights, sounds, and smells of the Bible's story be brought to life, but also the enduring truth must be clothed in fresh forms and images by the imaginative preacher. If in the succeeding steps of sermon preparation one is aware of the necessity of being helpful, truthful, and imaginative this balance is more likely to show up in a sermon. This is where the worksheet comes into play. Divide a legal size sheet as illustrated on page 66.

In the left-hand column I list in abbreviated form the names of people for whom I am praying. These names come from my counseling ministry, visitation, and other pastoral conversations. This list also includes abbreviations for events and issues that are also matters of prayerful concern. These concerns are a summons to the sermon to be helpful, but *first* a reminder that God is our well-proven help (Ps. 46:1). The top half of the worksheet is used for my exegetical notes. First the setting and background of the passage is summarized, then comes a verse-by-verse examination of the text.[9] Here previous notes on the text are edited and also condensed. On the bottom line of this section I try to state the theme or central theological idea as clearly as possible in one sentence. The second half of the page (two sheets of paper can be taped together if necessary) is the homiletical "response" to the

PRAYER CONCERNS	EXEGESIS
	(Theme)
	RESPONSE
	(Purpose)

text, and the pastoral context. Here are jotted down the images, visions, and problems arising from what is "heard."

Essentially the three sections of the paper are distinct and should not be homogenized. The prayer concerns should not intrude on the text before one has heard the Word coming through that particular passage. I find that listing such concerns keeps me from manipulating the text with a concern or need of which I am not *consciously* aware. Rather while hearing the text some of the concerns listed will be seen in a new light. Also the column on the left will grow with names of new people and concerns that seem to "appear" in the text. When insights born of the exegesis come to life they are placed in the lower half of the worksheet. For example, in discovering "the situation in life" of the text it may move one to note similarities or places of contact with the *Sitz im Leben* of the congregation. In translating or paraphrasing a sentence on the exegesis an image or metaphor may appear which could serve as a bridge to the truth of the text. This should be written down in the response section and evaluated later. When the exegesis is completed the idea or theme listed at the bottom of that half of the paper provides the guide for shaping the response material below it. When the idea that emerges from the text is now placed in the context of its present hearers, a purpose for the sermon will follow. A concise statement of the sermon purpose should be written on the bottom line of the worksheet.

On Thursday and Friday I allow the text to walk around with me while I am engaged in the constant variety of pastoral ministry.[10] As I do this with the theme and purpose of my sermon in mind, the body of the sermon begins to take shape. By the time I return to the study on Friday evening or Saturday morning the walk in the fresh air of pastoral rounds has trimmed some of the "fat" in the worksheet. I use red ink to underline the sections of the worksheet that are likely to be used in the sermon outline. This outline is the crucial step of bringing into control the scattered insights of the exegesis. The outline should fit the theme and purpose. Sometimes it consists of three or two major points with supporting material. Other times following the form of one of the parables it is a "sketch" for the retelling of that story. This is not the place for a detailed discussion of outlines. Basically it should be clear and possess essential unity and continuity.

My outline is written while I am "talking through" the sermon for the first time. From the beginning the goal is oral communication, therefore the shape of the sermon is governed by the ear rather than the eye. After an outline of fifty words or less I often prepare a full sermon manuscript. This allows me to be more precise in developing the central idea of the sermon. Also it is a check to see if the outline is adequate for moving the sermon toward its purpose. If the entire sermon is not written out, then I do write out certain portions, especially the introduction and the conclusion.

The introduction seeks to immediately involve the listeners. This means sometimes beginning with a problem presently troubling individuals and/or society—but not always. Often a good introduction begins with the text. Beginning with the text is not a wooden recital of a day in the life of the ancient Jebusites. The human drama of the Bible should be so lifelike that the listener can hardly turn away.

If the then-and-there, here-and-now quality of the biblical story has captivated the pastor in his or her preparation, it can be communicated with genuine enthusiasm to the congregation. This enthusiasm is not mindless or artificial excitement. Rather the pastor speaks as one who is addressed by a living Word. When that Word is judgment on unfaithfulness and inhumanity the shepherd (pastor) stands under that judgment. Likewise a Word of grace can be preached because it has been heard in all its costliness and winsomeness by the pastor-preacher. We are able to feed the sheep as we are fed by Christ and his community. Our style in preaching is to evidence the vulnerability of one sent out as a lamb. We cannot separate ourselves with a lofty pulpit manner or a dialect of piety unrelated to the world. There is a risk in appearing before people as one who hurts, doubts, and fails. It can be an affected style and used to manipulate people. Yet this vulnerability and standing with people under the judgment and grace of God is essential to pastoral preaching.

Not only must overly pious language be pruned, but also the speech of intellectual self-justification. My identity is not rooted in knowing theological or psychological terms that others do not. Nor can I be afraid of raising the questions from the text, pastoral conversations, and my own mind even if the answers are not yet as strong or as convincing as I would like. Saying this I am also aware that currently in some circles there is a glorification of "living the questions." Although living with our doubt and uncertainty *is* necessary; neither question nor answer is our final goal, but faith. This is faith that can live the questions without despair, and the answers without pride.

Sermon delivery in pastoral preaching is not limited to one method. A pastoral preacher may indeed (and many do) stand behind a pulpit and rely on a manuscript. That was my style for the first two or three years of preaching. This evolved into reducing my manuscript into a page of notes. In the last few years this style has taken a new turn. I begin to deliver the sermon from the middle of the chancel, away from the pulpit. The effect on the congregation's participation in the sermon was noticeable. I believe it has been a small physical reminder of the shepherd's position with the people. There are dangers. It is a fearful experience to be sans notes before a congregation; there is a feeling of nakedness. Charles Brown was honest, if a bit dramatic, when he said: "When I undertook to preach without a manuscript, I was beaten with rods of mortification, again and again I suffered shipwreck."[11] It is true crucial phrases can be forgotten, other phrases and words repeated too frequently. Yet my own experience is that those problems can be worked on and at least partially overcome. A man who had been preaching for twenty years told me that now when he preaches in this style, the congregation is with him when he has to walk back to his notes on the pulpit and retrieve a thought that has escaped him.

There is also the danger that this style can become the focal point rather than the preaching of the Word. If so it should be abandoned or modified. Wayne Oates sees pastoral preaching as implying a "conversational eye contact, and extemporaneous delivery."[12] My own experience seconds that. Yet no style of delivery, theory of preparation, or dependence on any lectionary should stand in the way of the Shepherd proclaiming the truth for the "good of souls."

CHAPTER V

Three Pastoral Sermons

Pastoral sermons are meant to be preached and heard, not published and read. This is not to say that published or printed sermons are without a pastoral purpose. Indeed, one deacon developed a pastoral ministry from distributing and, in some cases, reading aloud transcripts of his pastor's sermons to people in various nursing homes. My own reading regularly includes the sermons of men and women who are "pastoral preachers." Nonetheless, the printed sermon is necessarily "out of context." What becomes diluted is "the power of the relational." H. H. Farmer reminds us: ". . . that the act of preaching is part of a larger system of personal relationships and cannot be rightly understood in separation from it. The preacher, his sermon and his hearers are embedded in the larger system and what the preaching effects largely depends upon it."[1]

This larger system of personal relationships reveals itself only partially in the printed sermon. For not only the words, but also pauses, nervous laughter, facial expressions, all have meaning in the relationship of people and pastor in the sermon event. The pastoral sermon is also set within the relationship of people and pastor to the fullness of the biblical revelation. It is not a Word spoken out of season. The Word proclaimed *this* day is given shape by the pattern of scripture readings and biblical sermons that follow the church year.

Given then the serious limitations of printed pastoral

71

sermons, I will at least attempt to put the following sermons in their pastoral and liturgical context. They're not offered as models. Hopefully, it *can* be said that each was preached "as a part of a pastoral relationship, one activity of a settled and continuous ministry."[2]

1. FIFTH SUNDAY AFTER EPIPHANY

Pastoral Setting

Much of the setting is reflected in the sermon itself. A well-publicized television drama was seen by many in the congregation this week. Although it was about the phenomenon of the "electronic church," it raised the question (already at work in me through the lectionary readings and my pastoral visitation) of ministry to those who suffer a string of "undeserved" setbacks.

The woman in the Gospel lesson is healed, and immediately she jumps up and goes about doing good. But what about those who don't jump up; who apparently are not "healed" or "delivered"? What of good Job who suffers one thing after another? I think of a man in the church who had "come to Jesus" and was brought back from the brink of despair. Yet since that turning point one awful plague after another has been visited on his house. To describe his situation would be to stand accused of confusing fiction with fact. What is the Good News for him and a surprising number of others in this congregation who endure a kind of "serial misery"? How do we respond to such misery? These are the questions which shaped the following sermon.

February 7, 1982

Job 7:1-4
Mark 1:29-39

One Thing After Another

This story from our Gospel lesson is told with Mark's characteristic lean, straightforward style. A woman (a

72

good woman we presume) is laid aside with the pain and delirium of a fever. Jesus, when summoned, strides quickly, confidently toward her. Without a word he touches her and immediately she is healed, and just as suddenly she is up and about serving others. We are not left to guess about the consequence of this healing. The followers of Jesus go out to bring to him those who are racked by unending pain, or possessed by dark fears and rages. It seemed as though the whole city was gathered at his doorstep and he healed and delivered many.

Wouldn't it seem that if Jesus were alive today as Christians claim he is, that such healing would not be just a thing of the past? Indeed if the Spirit of Christ is active today shouldn't we use every modern avenue including television to get his message across? This week the movie *Pray T.V.* left me with a *yes . . . but* answer to the question I just asked. In what appeared to be a fairly well-balanced and penetrating view of T.V. evangelism, one scene left an indelible mark on me. A young woman who has been passively watching an evangelist on T.V. suddenly jumps from her chair and screams: "Come to Jesus, come to Jesus *and everything will be all right!*" Her anger builds to a crescendo; she has been listening to the promises and thinking of her mother who lost her husband and their business. It has been one tragic loss after another. How could this happen to a good woman, a person of faith, one who has "come to Jesus"?

This scene raises a question that goes back beyond the advent of modern evangelism, beyond television, beyond the Gospel of Mark. What is being raised is the question of the righteous (those in right relationship with God) who suffer. It is the question of suffering. It is the question of Job.

It is a question that we, the Christian church, need to wrestle with. What is our response to be to that woman and her mother, good people who seem to suffer *one thing after another.* Our initial response is to try to give answers, to give comfort by explaining or telling of our experiences. Often our words cover a fear. We are afraid just to listen, to let the whole unedited story pour out; for we fear we will be inadequate to help, to give a significant answer. Yet that is the first thing we are called to do in the face of "undeserved" suffering . . . *listen.*

Notice that in the verses we have read Job does not yet address himself to God, but to Eliphaz. Job is saying you've missed the point. "I am not a theological problem to be solved, I am a person!" Job is caught up in "serial misery." That's my term for an uninvited chain of events that has us asking when will it all end. In a recent book on several types of grief, Wayne Oates of the University of Louisville Medical School describes one type as "grief without end." And if we have the sensitivity and courage to hear, we learn that there are many men and women who "live quiet lives of desperation"! Aging parents who require constant care, children whose physical or emotional disabilities require special attention, the loss of income, on and on. This does not come from the chronic complainers, but from those who say "nothing." But if we begin to listen with what Dr. Theodore Reik calls the "third ear," we begin to hear the pain below the surface.

If we listen to Job in this way we hear one who sees life as a forced march, conscripted labor, always waiting for some kind of relief that never comes. All these metaphors reflect the cry, "Who asked for this?" He is saying in essence, "I wrestle with the demons of the night waiting for day to come, then the naked meaninglessness of day makes me long for night."

In the face of this Eliphaz gives Job advice: "Submit to God, admit you have done something wrong." But what Job has longed for is not someone to speak about his suffering, with advice, but to have "compassion," literally, "to suffer with" him. That is the second thing we are called to do in the face of such suffering—to *suffer with* the person. Language is a barrier. This can sound maudlin and even patronizing. The poet Blake's sketch depicts more accurately what is called for when he draws the three friends of Job sitting silently and compassionately on Job's dung heap. I think we should retire the word "sharing" for a while. We preachers have encouraged its use and therefore, not surprisingly, churches are always "sharing." But understanding the biblical definition may lessen this word's use and heighten its meaning. For we have a share in one another's suffering as well as joy. We do not commiserate, but take on a share of the burden; part of the dung heap becomes ours. Do you remember in *Pray T.V.* when the seminarian prayed with the woman who was experiencing "one thing after another." His prayer was not neat and polished for air time. He struggles with her, himself, and God in his prayer.

To have compassion is more than giving aid. My parents have taken in some neighbors whose house was condemned, and who were without heat and electricity during a recent snowstorm. It reminded me that compassion is taking on at least a part of the plight another is experiencing. You give up some of your own comfort, acceptance, standing in the community, and perhaps even the approval of your own family.

Finally, I believe our response to those who suffer is to mediate the sustaining, healing power of Jesus Christ. For we are caught up in something larger than our own listening and compassion. For they point beyond themselves to the source of our caring. We see Job's lament through the lens of the "suffering God" who was in Jesus Christ. The Book of Job does not give an answer to the problem of suffering. But Job does stand finally in the presence of the Answerer: "My Redeemer liveth!"

We who gather in his name affirm Jesus not as one who suffered in vain, but whose prayer, life, death, and resurrection were redemptive. They elicit a real change in the earth and its people. Now I know that gathering at this table, we go hungering after a mystery. I cannot explain Christ's suffering for us, but I believe that here we see a God who heard our cries and groans, who suffered with and for us. Incompletely now and fully someday the stuff of suffering is redeemed—made into a new health and wholeness that we cannot demand on our own terms but may receive from the God who does not turn from suffering.

If we are to mediate that Redeemer to others it will take more than electronic media. It will take common folks like you and me willing to listen . . . have compassion . . . and point beyond ourselves . . . to say with our silent caring as well as our words . . .

My Redeemer liveth!

Amen.

2. EASTER

Pastoral Setting

To say "Easter Sunday" is to already say a great deal about the setting. Extra chairs are set up, an extra anthem is prepared, extra flowers are arranged. Are pastors being honest when they claim there is no expectation of an *extra* special sermon? Most of the pressure comes not from the inexplicable nature of the resurrection but from our experience-oriented culture that requires a sunnier, more upbeat celebration than last year. Each year these elements are a part of the setting, but this Easter another dimension seems to be present.

In my first three years as pastor here there was not one funeral for a church member. Now in the last several months many of us have known the suddenness of death and the lingering emptiness of grief. Two weeks ago a man who gave meaning to the word "elder" died. Not formally educated but "conversant" with the church fathers and mothers, steeped in biblical study, his quiet example was conspicuously absent this Easter. Another ingredient in the pastoral setting was the way in which terminal illness had taken new and frightening meaning. The reality of death had come to the young and middle-aged as well as to the elderly.

All of this called for a sermon based on the resurrection narrative, but from an angle of vision often neglected. The abrupt ending of Mark's Gospel provides a word of resurrection which is not glib or easy . . . it is a word that is not death-denying but is ultimately death-defeating.

April 11, 1982

Beyond the 'Ugsome' Reality

On this mountain the Lord of Hosts will prepare
a banquet of rich fare for all the peoples,
a banquet of wines well matured and richest fare,
well matured wines strained clear.
On this mountain the Lord will swallow up
that veil that shrouds all the peoples,
the pall thrown over all the nations;
he will swallow up death for ever.

(Isa. 25:6-7 NEB)

But go and give this message to his disciples and Peter; "He is going on before you into Galilee; there you will see him, as he told you." Then they went out and ran away from the tomb, beside themselves with terror. They said nothing to anybody, for they were afraid.

(Mark 16:7-8 NEB)

If Easter joy is a mood to be set, a feeling to be engendered, then we probably go about it in the right way: families and friends gathered, the easy congeniality of a church breakfast, and a sanctuary in bloom. Food and flowers. Banquets and bouquets. The symbols are not wrong, but is it more than a mood or a feeling after all? Is it possible to lose the resurrection in Easter?

Some time ago in Hawaii a Chinese man, following the tradition of his ancestors, brought a nine course meal to a cemetery for the "spirit" of a friend who had died. An American who was placing flowers on a grave witnessed this strange sight and said sarcastically, "When do you think your friend will come up and eat his food?" The Oriental gentleman smiled and answered, "Same time your friend comes up to smell your flowers."

Is it possible that the symbols of Easter can be used not to celebrate the costly victory of Christ over death, but as a denial of death? A man who lived several centuries ago has challenged me about this. His name was Miles Coverdale and he described death as "ugsome and very terrible." Unfortunately the word "ugsome" has slipped out of our language; but what a descriptive word. We recoil from its sound. We tremble in its presence. Something ugsome is not easily and mindlessly romanticized. Perhaps Mr. Coverdale lived in an age more shaped by biblical realism than our own. For the Bible does not apply cosmetic surgery to the face of death. In the Bible death is a reality physically and emotionally. Jesus' friend had been dead three days before he arrived, and the King James Version tells us that the dead man "stinketh." Equally important in describing the same incident, Jesus' feelings of loss and sadness are not hidden from view. Jesus wept. Perhaps C. S. Lewis, reeling from the loss of his wife, called death by its true names, "an appalling horror and a stinking indignity."

Isaiah reminds us that death is more than a private, individual matter, for there is a pall over all nations. The dictionary says that a "pall" is a "gloomy covering as in a pall of smoke." It does not take a great deal of imagination to see a mushroom-shaped cloud we deny and yet move toward at the same time.

In fact, our primary way of dealing with all kinds of
death is denial. It was again C. S. Lewis who told of one
young woman saying she never thought of death because
science would come up with something by then. Indeed
thirty years later some assert cryogenics (freezing and
unfreezing living bodies) is the answer. When will we
learn that we are all terminal? When will I admit it? It is
not morbid but the beginning of wisdom to insist that
until we face our own death we are not totally free to
live.

Isaiah, long before it was fashionable in Israel, spoke
of a reality beyond and through the "ugsome reality." In
the images of Hebrew poetry it is a great banquet, the
feast of everlasting life. It is not humanity swallowed up
by the grave, but death swallowed up by God. True, it
was described in words made familiar by a myth of
Baalism that spoke of Baal swallowing up the god
"death" (like a giant Pac-Man). Some understood it
simply as the death and rebirth of vegetation, the rites of
spring. Sound familiar? We too have a vague mystic sense
of immortality. It is a nice hopeful thought for Easter and
funerals, but is it terrible enough to swallow up the
ugsome reality of death?

In the New Testament it is more than a vague hope
that confronts us. It is no less than the strong Son of
God entering our weakness, our suffering, our death. *Yet
death is not the final reality.* It is Jesus who fulfills the
promise of a New Kingdom, the breaking in of the rule
and reign of God, spoken by Isaiah centuries before. In
him the loving purposes of God for all nations and all
time are revealed. But in the early morning air of that
first day all of this seems dead. Hope is dead. Jesus is
dead. The women who loved him most and shared his
great vision now come, not expectantly, but with the
resolve of loving duty. They are left with only the
"ugsome reality" but nonetheless face that reality and

79

come to anoint the dead body. Their faith and love have equipped them to do what must be done.

Some of you know I am hopelessly addicted to a radio show that airs on Saturday night. I wish the fictitious sponsors of the show were real products. One of my favorites is "Powdermilk Biscuits." They are made especially for shy people and they promise to enable shy people to "get up and do what must be done." We are not bold or extravagant in our faith. A bit shy, we would settle for the power to do what must be done. Let's not put that down, for it is a great gift to have strength (if not enthusiasm) to do our duty in an overwhelming situation.

Here their best, their human action, "We are looking for him" is met *and transcended* by God's action. The word of the messenger breaks in: "He is risen. He is not here; he has gone before you into Galilee." What was their reaction? Hallelujah? Hosanna? Eureka? No. (I love the realism of the Bible.) It was terror, bewilderment. Their response was a dread that something overwhelmingly unthinkable had actually happened. This trembling awe is always the human response in Mark's Gospel when the holy is revealed, when God acts. If the resurrection actually did sneak up on us and its reality swallowed up our smashed hopes and our deadly attitudes, what would be our response? It takes something that "terrific" to swallow up that which we deny and yet are a slave to . . . "death *is* ugsome and very terrible."

Only the resurrection of God's Holy One can transform death into life, rejection into love. "O Death, where is your victory?" (I Cor. 15:55 NEB). The banquet of life is ours, Isaiah's vision is wondrously won in Christ's death for us. Yet if we stand with these women in the terror of that wonderful moment will we ever again be able to glibly say, "Death is swallowed up in victory," without knowing the terrible cost of it all?

There have been several times in the past few years when I have awakened in the middle of the night with a start, even with an irrepressible yell. My dream, however vague the detail, wasn't about death. The fear that I experienced was not so much being scared of death but being *scared to death* of a reality greater than I could imagine. For when I woke I was overwhelmed by the awesome promise of eternal life to those who believe. It boggles the mind. Broken relationships, crib death, the demons of war, *nothing* can separate us from the love of God in Christ. Only when we, like the women at the tomb, know the terribleness of the resurrection can we know its everlasting comfort.

Then the words can come to you and me, "Fear not!" "He is not here." If he is the Lord of life then death has not defeated him and we are led away from the tomb back into "Galilee." "Galilee" is the place where we work (frenetically or listlessly) and live (with less than perfect people) and have our being (endlessly questioned). But it is the very place where we are called to be witnesses to the resurrection. Life is no longer measured by how long we live but for whom. We are not to be lingering around the tomb but to go back where the Risen Lord sends us, to "Galilee." "To Peter." For Peter is the one who messed up, and whom we have successfully isolated from the community. There are those like Peter who are experiencing a "living death": the ugsome reality of guilt, failure, and defeat. To them we are "to go and give this message. . . ."

Amen.

3. FIRST SUNDAY AFTER PENTECOST (TRINITY)

Pastoral Setting

In a sermon feedback session a woman said candidly, "We are told constantly in church to go and do good in a world of overwhelming pain and evil. But we are sent out without the resources and the vision needed to sustain us." Last week's scripture lesson (Joel 2:28-32) promised powerful visions for male *and* female, young *and* old. This Sunday we see the disillusioned Isaiah turned around by a vision of the Holy One of Israel. Thoroughly modern and seemingly skeptical people are yearning for an experience of the transcendent. More and more of my counseling appointments deal with questions about prayer, meditation, and worship. The question often comes from people who thought they were "past" such concerns. Also, "The Forum" of our church, which usually centers on social and political issues, asked me to come this month and speak about worship.

These incidents and others move into the interface between a search for personal meaning, a sense of the transcendent, and a call to minister to the world and its institutions. A few weeks before this sermon was preached I attended a convocation on preaching, sponsored by two conferences of The United Methodist Church. At the convocation Dr. Edmund Steimle insisted that the fabric of the biblical witness is thoroughly *secular*. This does not negate but heightens the transcendent Word, which comes through the secular language and setting. He gave as an example the biblical passage which soars to spiritual heights from a political situation: "In the year that King Uzziah died I saw the Lord."

June 10, 1979   Isaiah 6:1-8

"In the Year. . . ."

"In the year that King Uzziah died I saw the Lord!"

Is this escapist literature we are reading? Six-winged creatures, smoke, foundations shaking. Is this some kind of synthetic high induced to dull the pain of reality? No! This is the only language capable of describing the vision which transformed the life of Isaiah. Last week on Pentecost Sunday we celebrated the promise of the Holy Spirit: all ages, sexes, classes of people will dream dreams and see visions. The promise is not of ideal dreams and selfish visions. It is the ability to go beyond the borders of our own insights and glimpse a portion of the eternal reality. When and how does this happen to us? God's Spirit cannot be grafted on a neat and tidy flow chart. The wind blows where she wills. Yet, this re-creative breath often fills us when we are most disillusioned with human plans and dreams.

This may well have been the experience of Isaiah. One scholar described the fifty-two-year reign of King Uzziah as a time of *prosperity* and *progress*. Suddenly the king is dead! Imagine the impact on a patriotic young man like Isaiah. The weight of mortality and the limits of all human institutions came crashing in upon him. In the early 1960s many of us learned to sing the praises of the "New Frontier." We lived in a hopeful, optimistic era. Progress was our most important product. With ingenuity, enthusiasm, *and* the right leadership we could surely do anything.

"In the year John F. Kennedy died. . . ."

Painfully we began to see the limits of progress and unbounded hope in our future.

If our age has been marked by the reign of progress, no less have we worshiped prosperity. Paul Simon's song "Have a Good Time" reveals the "stuff" our dreams are made of:

> So God bless the goods we was given,
> And God bless the U S of A
> And God bless our standard of livin'
> Let's keep it that way
> And we'll all have a good time.

It is our prosperity that we worship and not a thrice Holy God, high and lifted up.

In this year of runaway inflation will we see the Lord? Only if we can see past the gods of science and technology. We continue to trust in our ingenuity to bring the return of progress and unbridled prosperity. A recent issue of *Saturday Review* focused on a hundred years of our love affair with science and technology. The positive aspects of "the affair" were clearly pointed out. Nonetheless one writer declared, "Until very recently in this heady century we tended to emphasize the blessings of science and technology, to accept the benefits without much question, while paying little attention to the risks." In the year of Three Mile Island our confidence died. Technology is not inherently evil, but neither is it God. "Whatever thy heart clings to and relies upon that properly is thy God." So said Luther.

Young Isaiah returned to the Temple with a heavy heart. He could cling no longer to the security provided by the nation and its leaders. For Isaiah and others there was no doubt a turning from the gods that failed. Where could they turn? We can picture Isaiah's going once again to the Temple, hoping against hope that behind the familiar form and ritual reality could be found.

Honesty compels us to admit that not every anthem and sermon is a burning bush aflame with the glory of God. During much of the worship service our minds are engaged elsewhere. A couple of weeks ago I discovered a worship bulletin that had been scribbled on. Next to the symbol of the burning bush on the cover were the words "Noxzema" and "razor blades." I laughed out loud when I read those hastily scrawled reminders. How many times in prayer or worship my mind has drifted to the most mundane matters. Isaiah could not have been immune to such experiences. Yet this time every window of his soul was opened to God. Perhaps at such moments it is not so much our finding God, but the Holy moving in on us. We are ready.

Three Pastoral Sermons

His train fills the Temple. . . .

In seeing the Lord high and lifted up we are able to see ourselves clearly, perhaps for the first time. In the presence of the Holy we are a people of unclean lips: the purest human speech falls short of holiness. An experience of God's presence therefore brings forth from us confession. Fortunately you and I are not left there; for in our worship this morning the assurance of pardon follows the prayer of confession. This is not a meaningless ritual. Once we experience the gap that exists between a holy, righteous God and a people of unclean lips we are able to see the bridge that spans the chasm. Emmanuel is not only God with us, but for us. In his life of holy obedience and a death of sacrificial love we can know not only the presence of God, but God's forgiveness as well. It is a mystery that surpasses all the theories and formulas. "In Jesus Christ we are forgiven." We are freed to dream the dreams and follow the visions of God's Holy Spirit.

So is this the message: "Fly to the bosom of God—retreat from the nasty realm of politics, commerce, and technology"? Are we to escape the twentieth century and seek to be first-century Christians? No! True worship is never an escape. In seeking the ultimate we are seeking the One who is worthy to name and rule *all* of life. When, like doubting Thomas we can proclaim, "My Lord and my God," we have learned how to worship. Worship is not a retreat from life, it is the renewing of life, the reordering of life. A. N. Whitehead in *Science and the Modern World* said, "The worship of God is not a rule of safety—it is an adventure of the spirit." Yes, adventure. When God is made known to us it is so we might hear the accompanying call: "Whom shall I send, and who will go for us?"

"In the year that King Uzziah died I saw the Lord!"

—— CHAPTER VI ——

An Annotated Bibliography

Developing a Pastoral Theology

Andrews, Charles Freer. *The Good Shepherd.* New York: Harper & Brothers, 1940.

The "devotional" emphasis of this work (originally the University Lectures in Pastoral Theology at Cambridge in 1937) might discourage the reader from serious investigation. That would be a loss. The author's keen mind, social concern, and pastoral heart, produces a book that is warm and wise. C. F. Andrews, missionary, scholar, was first a Christian shepherd.

Baxter, Richard. *The Reformed Pastor.* Grand Rapids: Sovereign Grace Press, 1971.

This or one of the other abridged editions of Baxter's pastoral classic (the original was some seven hundred pages) should be read by those who wish to understand the discipline and tenderness required of a shepherd of the flock. The book, written in 1656, is an exposition of Acts 20:28 and a plea for pastoral responsibility.

Beazley, George, Jr., et al. "What Is Your Concept of Pastoral Theology?" *Religion in Life* 28 (Autumn 1959): 512-25.

Ten pastors responded to the above question with predictable variety. Some rephrased Hiltner, others spoke in terms of counseling or worship. The last two responses by Samuel Miller and Chester Pennington offer the most beneficial insights into a pastoral *theology* for preaching as well as counseling.

Bernanos, Georges. *The Diary of a Country Priest.* Translated by Pamela Morris. New York: Macmillan, 1937.

Both the humanity and the nobility of the pastoral office are vividly drawn in this moving novel. There is a deep understanding of the Word of God going beyond "comfortable truths." "Truth is meant to save you first and the comfort comes afterwards." Yet this truth is brought forward with pastoral concern, "when the Lord has drawn from me some word for the good of souls, I know, because of the pain of it" (p. 54).

Boyce, Greer W. "Pastoral Theology Today." *Canadian Journal of Theology* 6 (January 1960): 31-34.

This article explores pastoral theology as reflection on the distinctive roles of a pastor relating to persons. It is also helpful in calling attention to the danger of pastoral theology being dominated by psychology. (See page 34 for pastoral theology's effect on preaching.)

Clebsch, William A., and Jaekle, Charles R. *Pastoral Care in Historical Perspective.* Englewood Cliffs, N.J.: Prentice-Hall, 1964.

Here is one of the few books on the history of pastoral care. Their approach is to begin with definitions, historical overview, then four major functions of pastoral care. The four functions are then illustrated by primary source data. (The inclusion of the reconciling function is helpful and can be applied creatively to preaching.)

Clifford, Paul Rowntree. *The Pastoral Calling.* Great Neck, N.Y.: Channel Press, 1961.

This book does not add much to a theology of pastoral ministry, although the first three chapters give a good basic outline of a Reformed (Baptist) view of pastoral ministry. Clifford's theology helps him go beyond adjustment to life counseling and preaching. Of interest is his call to go beyond the expository-topical debate in preaching and see the story form as the foundation of Christian preaching (p. 60).

Davies, Horton. *A Mirror of the Ministry in Modern Novels.* New York: Oxford University Press, 1959.

The world of fiction is a rich source for developing a pastoral perspective. Since it is impossible to list all the works of fiction that deal with the Christian pastor, I would recommend Dr. Davies' book as an excellent introduction to some novels written in the first half of this century that give us a variety of views on the minister. Of special interest is the generally critical treatment of the Protestant preacher-evangelist (pp. 21-50) and the very positive view of the Catholic director of souls (pp. 81-110) in the books treated.

Greenslade, Stanley Lawrence. *Shepherding the Flock*. London: S.C.M. Press, 1967.

The Oxford historian S. L. Greenslade has given us a historical perspective on the problems of pastoral discipline in the early church and in the emerging churches today (i.e., Third-World countries). This slim volume makes a solid contribution to American church people who have tended to neglect this tough but important side of pastoral care and preaching.

Gregory I, the Great, Saint. *Pastoral Care*. Translated by Henry Davis, S. J. Westminster, Md.: The Newman Press, 1955.

Modern developmental and social psychology have made us aware of the difficulty of preaching to one congregation made up of divergent personalities in varying stages of development. Here one of the church fathers tries to deal as pastor and preacher with these shades of difference. There is pastoral balance in the words of Gregory I; he is not afraid to "comfort the afflicted or afflict the comfortable" (i.e., p. 182).

Hartman, Olov. *Earthly Things*. Translated by Eric J. Sharpe. Grand Rapids: Eerdmans Publishing Co., 1968.

Rev. Hartman is a well-known Swedish novelist and dramatist. What is not as well known is that he teaches pastoral psychology at Uppsala and has made a substantial contribution to our understanding of pastoral theology which may accept psychology as an ally but finds its roots in the history, scripture, and sacraments of the church (pp. 130-31). The essays, "The Minister as Pastor" and "The Pastoral Aspect of Preaching" are especially helpful for our present study.

Hiltner, Seward. "Freedom and Tradition in Pastoral Theology." *Princeton Seminary Bulletin* 56 (October 1962): 33-41.

This is a clear call for pastoral theology to reflect on the concrete experience of ministry. Preaching is but one area that does not need more technique but serious theological reflection, according to Hiltner.

————. *Preface to Pastoral Theology*. Nashville: Abingdon Press, 1958.

"*Preface* . . ." is generally considered a pioneering work in pastoral theology. Hiltner makes a strong case for pastoral theology as a legitimate branch of theology. It brings a theological view to the work of ministry and then gathers data from the work of ministry for the rethinking of theology. More study in the relationship of the shepherding and communicating perspective would be helpful for pastoral preaching.

―――. *The Christian Shepherd: Some Aspects of Pastoral Care.* Nashville: Abingdon Press, 1959.

Here Hiltner's definition of shepherding as "solicitous tender and individualized care" is developed in the framework of modern pastoral psychology. Unfortunately the relationship of judgment and love in "shepherding" is merely mentioned and not developed.

Hofmann, Hans. "Making the Ministry Relevant in Our Time." *Religion in Life* 28 (Autumn 1959): 483-93.

This article emphasizes the critical role of pastoral theology and its need to go beyond an academic approach to theology (p. 492). An important contribution is his criticism of the "shepherding" model in pastoral theology.

Jansen, John F. "The Pastoral Image in the New Testament." *Austin Seminary Bulletin* XCIV (May 1979): 13-21.

Dr. Jansen has provided us with a brief but sound overview of the biblical metaphor of shepherd. There is a compelling argument for the "shepherd-sheep" mixed metaphor as avoiding the danger of a superior-inferior relationship within the church. The exposition of I Peter 5:1-4 is most helpful.

Jefferson, Charles E. *The Minister as Shepherd.* New York: Thomas Y. Crowell, 1912.

The vision of living in a universe created by a Shepherd God permeates Jefferson's pastoral theology. The shepherding ministry must include God's work through us of watching, guarding, guiding, healing, feeding, and loving. This rich understanding of pastoral ministry has some exciting possibilities for the twentieth-century church.

Kemp, Charles F. *A Pastoral Triumph.* New York: Macmillan, 1949.

This book by a well-known advocate of pastoral preaching should be read with one of the modern abridgments of Baxter's *The Reformed Pastor*. It is clear that preaching as a "dying man to dying men" comes from one who "takes heed to all the flock."

Lapsley, James N., Jr. "Pastoral Theology: Its Nature, Methods, and Uses." *Princeton Seminary Bulletin* 1 (1977): 21-34.

Lapsley's inaugural address discusses some of the major ways of "doing pastoral theology." There is a strong emphasis on the context of pastoral theology in the institutional church (i.e., p. 29). Of importance to pastoral preaching is his example of pastoral theology using its resources to work through theological categories such as God's judgment.

————. "Pastoral Theology Past and Present." *The New Shape of Pastoral Theology,* edited by William B. Oglesby, Jr. Nashville: Abingdon Press, 1969, pp. 31-48.

This, in my opinion, is the best short summary in the field of pastoral theology. Also important is his emphasis on the *data of ministry.*

McNeill, John T. *The History of the Cure of Souls.* New York: Harper & Brothers, 1951.

This is an excellent history of pastoral care before the "age of modern psychology." There is however almost no mention of preaching as a part of the cure of souls.

Oden, Thomas C. *Agenda for Theology.* New York: Harper & Row, 1979.

This is a most unusual book. Oden, who has often been associated with several modern movements in theology and psychology, is calling for a recovery of our theological roots in "ancient ecumenical Christianity." Building upon this foundation Oden has high hopes for the pastor as theologian. From this view comes a chapter on "the craft of pastoral guardianship." With the proliferation and power of cults today can we ignore the pastoral role of "guardianship"?

Osborn, Ronald E. *In Christ's Place: Christian Ministry in Today's World.* St. Louis: Bethany Press, 1967.

Osborn has done a commendable job in this book of exploring the biblical-theological foundation of the Christian ministry. His chapter on the shepherd image is well worth the reading by all who would understand the depth and staying power of this metaphor. Like Rudolf Bohren, this author explores the importance of a shepherding community for truly pastoral ministry (p. 123).

Peck, George. "Of Sheep and Shepherds." *Andover Newton Quarterly* 19 (November 1978): 105-10.

In sermonic form this professor of theology calls for an image of shepherding that goes beyond "a mutual hand holding society" (p. 109). This is a compelling call for restoring strength and compassion, content and style to the rich biblical image of shepherd.

Peterson, Eugene H. *Five Smooth Stones for Pastoral Work.* Atlanta: John Knox Press, 1980.

This is the most stimulating of the recently published books which relate biblical resources to pastoral care. This exegetical and historical work on the Megilloth of the Old Testament makes their use as pastoral tools quite credible. From these five scrolls Peterson develops the themes of prayer directing, storytelling, pain sharing, nay saying, and community building. Throughout, aspects of pastoral care seldom addressed are given fresh biblical insights.

This dissertation provides a detailed, careful study of the concept of shepherding in the Bible. What is most helpful is that his four main ingredients of shepherding cover the breath of the pastoral perspective. This study is a real asset for pastoral preaching.

Thornton, Edward E. *Theology and Pastoral Counseling.* Englewood Cliffs, N.J.: Prentice-Hall, 1964.

Thornton uses Bonhoeffer's understanding of the ultimate (justification by faith) and the penultimate (everything that aids in providing the route over which God travels in coming to men and women). This is a needed warning that pastoral counseling and preaching-worship as penultimates can stand in the way of the ultimate.

Thurneysen, Eduard. *A Theology of Pastoral Care.* Translated by Jack A. Worthington et al. Atlanta: John Knox Press, 1962.

This book is heavily influenced by a Barthian theological perspective. Thurneyson has a high view of preaching. His view of pastoral care as "healing conversation" has implications for preaching as well as counseling. For him one aspect of caring is to faithfully proclaim the Word of God (p. 66).

Underwood, Ralph L. "Pastoral Care and the Office of the Pastor." *Austin Seminary Bulletin* XCIV (May 1979): 5-12.

In an age when "pastoral" has become synonymous with "personal counseling" this article seeks a middle view of the pastor proclaiming the Word of God verbally, sacramentally, and in caring service. Also there is a healthy emphasis on the total pastoral community with ordained pastors responsible for "pastoral oversight" (p. 6).

Way, Peggy. "Pastoral Dimensions of Administration: An Invitation to Be Pastoral Theologians." Speech given at Scarritt College, Nashville, September 8, 1977.

The speech examines the "pastoral act" in the light of pastoral theology. The emphasis on specific acts viewed from the whole is helpful for the preacher who must be pastoral as well as prophetic.

Williams, Daniel Day. *The Minister and the Care of Souls.* New York: Harper & Row, 1961. Reprint, 1977.

Here a theologian takes several key theological concepts such as salvation, authority, grace, and reprocesses them through the perspective of pastoral theology.

Winter, Gibson. "Pastoral Counseling *or* Pastoral Care." *Pastoral Psychology* 8 (February 1957): 16-24.

Winter offers a timely reminder that the community of faith is a part of pastoral care; one to one is not the only model for caring.

Pastoral Approach to Preaching

Books

Abbey, Merril R. *Communication in Pulpit and Parish.* Philadelphia: The Westminster Press, 1973.

This book is an aid to building a theology of pastoral preaching. Abbey, using the language of communication research, calls for preaching to encode its message only after decoding the biblical documents and people's needs (pp. 99, 126-27). The pastor "does theology less as an academic question and more as a search for light on the shadowed place he has found in the troubled lives of the people" (p. 127). Also the three practical suggestions for increasing the preacher's power to listen are excellent (pp. 61-62).

Babin, David E. *Week In-Week Out: A New Look at Liturgical Preaching.* New York: The Seabury Press, 1976.

Babin emphasizes speaking to people's needs with the fullness of the gospel ("gospelling," pp. 71-72). Yet he adds a less familiar dimension to the understanding of pastoral preaching when he develops the idea of "celebrating health" in chapter nine. Another element here that is lacking in much of pastoral preaching is the assurance that some things are better said in the liturgy than in the sermon.

Bartlett, Gene E. *The Audacity of Preaching.* New York: Harper & Row, 1964.

Based on the 1961 Beecher lectures, this book has several creative suggestions for pastoral preaching including an emphasis on the laity's role (pp. 44-45), and viewing the pastor as prophet (pp. 125-26). The "idea of a scholarship of involvement" (pp. 67-71) makes a good case for theology being worked out in a pastoral context.

————. *The Authentic Pastor.* Valley Forge, Pa.: Judson Press, 1978.

There is some excellent material here for building a pastoral approach to preaching, although it seems to be scattered at random throughout the book. Bartlett doesn't go into the issue in depth but does identify resources for pastoral care that go beyond the psychological model (pp. 31ff.). He touches on pastoral preaching as disclosure, insight, word of hope, and sacrament.

Beverly, Harry Black. *Harry Emerson Fosdick's Pedigt weise, Its Significance (for America), Its Limits, Its Overcoming.* Winterthur, Switzerland: Verlag P. G. Keller, 1965.

Despite its cumbersome title this book is a challenging, critical study of Fosdick's "preaching as counseling," and a call to go beyond it. He gives examples of pastoral preachers who are also biblical expositors.

Blackwood, Andrew W. *Doctrinal Preaching for Today.* Nashville: Abingdon Press, 1956.

Dr. Blackwood touches on another neglected area of pastoral preaching . . . solid theological content addressed to real needs. In his simple, straightforward manner he makes a solid case for going beyond the "cult of reassurance." Chapter 5, "The Doctrine in Pulpit Counseling" is especially helpful.

Bohren, Rudolf. *Preaching and Community.* Translated by David E. Green. Atlanta: John Knox Press, 1966.

This is an excellent book for developing a pastoral approach to theology and for thinking theologically about pastoral ministry. Bohren sees preaching and pastoral care as ministries of the community of faith and gives concrete examples of how this works itself out in the life of the pastor and congregation. This series of essays goes a long way in broadening and deepening one's understanding of pastoral preaching.

Brister, C. W. *Pastoral Care in the Church.* New York: Harper & Row, 1964.

A Baptist minister and seminary professor offers valuable assistance in pastoral preaching. The chapter on theological perspectives is clearly written and gives a good summary of some of the major motifs in pastoral theology. His definition of pastoral preaching is in my opinion one of the most balanced to be found in current literature (pp. 118, 125-26).

Brooks, Phillips. *Eight Lectures on Preaching.* London: S.P.C.K., 1959.

This reprint of a classic on preaching should be read more than once by anyone interested in pastoral preaching. One hundred years later the author's statement about the work of the pastor and the preacher belonging together (pp. 75ff.) remains the most lucid description of the creative tension generated between these two roles.

Brown, Charles Reynolds. *The Art of Preaching.* New York: Macmillan, 1922.

This course of Yale lectures indirectly makes a strong case for pastoral preaching. Implicit in these lectures is a dynamic process similar to the one we have been advocating: (a) in knowing the spiritual, moral, social needs of the people he or she pastors, the preacher *visualizes* the congregation as the sermon is prepared (p. 16); (b) the fullness of God's pastoral care comes through a systematic program of biblical preaching (p. 46); and (c) this pastoral-biblical approach moves the preacher to an open, direct, personal *style* of preaching (pp. 84-85).

Browne, R. E. C. *The Ministry of the Word.* Philadelphia: Fortress Press, 1976.

Wallace Fisher asserts, "this theological study can be reread profitably every three to five years." (*Who Dares to Preach?* p. 194). Indeed it is a solid, enduring work that gives us an artistic vision of pastoral preaching as imaginative.

Capps, Donald. *Pastoral Counseling and Preaching: A Quest for an Integrated Ministry.* Philadelphia: The Westminster Press, 1980.

In a previous book Capps developed a thematic approach to pastoral care by using four key elements: identification of the problem, reconstruction of the problem (cause and context), diagnostic interpretation, and pastoral intervention. In this book the author attempts to integrate preaching and counseling as "formally structured acts of ministry," using these common elements.

It is possible to have some questions about these elements as an integrating system for ministry yet to benefit from the very helpful and thought-provoking analysis of theological diagnosis

An Annotated Bibliography

in preaching and counseling (pp. 89-90). This is a book worth reading.

Cleland, James T. *Preaching to Be Understood*. Nashville: Abingdon Press, 1965.

Dr. Cleland's call for "bifocal preaching" (through exegesis of the scripture and people's needs) is not new. It is, nonetheless, clearly written with enough force to inspire better vision in the would-be preacher. This is, however, not the book for fresh insights into pastoral preaching.

Coffin, Henry Sloane. *What to Preach*. New York: Harper & Brothers, 1926.

In using the term "pastoral preaching," Coffin means one of the five main types of preaching. Yet in reading the chapter on this topic one discovers a view that undergirds all preaching. Here is the Bible interpreting life, and life giving urgency to the message of the Bible (p. 121).

Cox, James W. *A Guide to Biblical Preaching*. Nashville: Abingdon Press, 1976.

This book emphasizes the Bible as the pastor's most "life-centered" resource (p. 28). Cox, as a Baptist, sees the pastoral importance of lectionary preaching even for the less formally liturgical churches.

Crocker, Lionel, ed. *Harry Emerson Fosdick's Art of Preaching: An Anthology*. Springfield, Ill.: Charles C. Thomas, Publisher, 1971.

Dr. Crocker has rendered us a service by putting several of Fosdick's most important essays on preaching in one volume, including: "What Is the Matter with Preaching?" and "Personal Counseling and Preaching." Also included are excellent articles by Robert Clark, Charles Kemp, Crocker, and others that shed light on Fosdick's style of pastoral preaching.

Erdahl, Lowell O. *Preaching for the People*. Nashville: Abingdon Press, 1976.

From the viewpoints of the listener and preacher this is a brief treatment of the basics of preaching: why, what, how. The "how" includes a prophetic-social element that is often excluded from pastoral-personal preaching. On page sixty-five there is an excellent statement of prophetic preaching expressing pastoral concern.

Farmer, Herbert H. *The Servant of the Word*. Philadephia: Fortress Press, 1964.

This is a small but powerful tool for working out a truly pastoral theology of preaching. Farmer applies Buber's

95

"I-Thou" to the relationship between preacher and listener. He gives great importance to the pastoral relationship in preaching as opposed to the concept of "guest speaker."

Fisher, Wallace E. *Who Dares to Preach? The Challenge of Biblical Preaching.* Minneapolis: Augsburg Publishing House, 1979.

Dr. Fisher offers a preaching perspective that will inform and energize the minister despite changing fads and opinions. This perspective is firmly rooted in a vision of the preacher as shepherd, "He and she recognize and accept that authentic ministry does not originate in the pastor's strong intellect, affable disposition, personal attractiveness, gregarious nature, or good digestive system. Authentic ministry centers in Christ. Shepherds care for people because Christ cares for them, motivating and equipping them to care for others" (p. 65).

Ford, D. W. Cleverly. *The Ministry of the Word.* Grand Rapids: Eerdmans Publishing Co., 1979.

The author was by all accounts a gifted and faithful pastor-preacher for over forty years. Neither the scope of his theology or pastoral concern can be called narrow. This is most evident here in his discussion of "preaching in the worshipping community" and in the chapter "The Word of Wisdom."

―――. *A Pastoral Preacher's Notebook.* London: Hodder Stoughton, 1965.

Father Ford sees pastoral preaching through the Episcopal tradition: "Anglican ministry undertakes preaching as one way, among others, of executing the 'cure of souls' . . . Preaching must be a part of the shepherding undergirded by prayer" (p. 13). More about this perspective would have been helpful. The main purpose of this book was to complete a trilogy of sermon anthologies emphasizing in turn: expository, theological, and pastoral preaching. The lasting value of Ford's sermons is that they are (each one) biblical, theological, and pastoral.

Forsyth, P. T. *Positive Preaching and the Modern Mind.* Grand Rapids: Eerdmans Publishing Co., 1964.

Unfortunately even this paperback reprint of the 1907 Beecher lecture is out of print. His pastoral spirit is evident throughout, and despite its date, the book is indeed "modern" in its understanding of the place of preaching within "the press and care of life."

Fosdick, Harry Emerson. *The Living of These Days.* New York: Harper & Brothers, 1956.

This is the autobiography of the famous exponent of life-situation preaching. It is helpful to see how Fosdick came to view preaching as a form of counseling. He tells how his preaching was shaped by modern biblical criticism and the needs of human life.

Fuller, Reginald H. *The Use of the Bible in Preaching.* Philadelphia: Fortress Press, 1981.

The genius of this book is that it offers so much help in so few pages to those who would preach pastorally, biblically, and liturgically (see pages 35-40). In pastoral preaching workshops there are often requests for aids in "getting through a text to a sermon." Here are step-by-step suggestions (pp. 21-33, 43-50) that are clear, solid, and yet flexible.

Hiltner, Seward. *Ferment in the Ministry.* Nashville: Abingdon Press, 1969.

Hiltner's chapter on "The Ministry as Preaching" is not as clear as one might like. Nonetheless his distinction between pastoral care and preaching avoids the common notion that one is but an application of the other.

Howe, Reuel. *Partners in Preaching.* New York: The Seabury Press, 1967.

Howe stresses the community aspect of preaching and the need to see the sermon not simply as the preacher's work (p. 102), but dialogue.

Jabusch, Willard F. *The Person in the Pulpit: Preaching as Caring.* Nashville: Abingdon Press, 1980.

This is not as tightly knit a treatise on preaching as an expression of caring as one might want, but the strong pastoral base cannot be doubted. Although some chapters seem to be wayside stops along the main theme, they are refreshing stops. This is especially true of the chapter on "Voices of the Pioneers." The pastoral temerity of Saint Bernard speaks to our own condition more redemptively than a dozen "current" books on pastoral care.

Jackson, Edgar N. *A Psychology for Preaching.* New York: Harper & Row, 1981.

There is much here that points to the wholistic approach of pastoral care . . . not just counseling. I do believe the conclusions from the poll of what people want to hear from the pulpit must be measured against the need for prophetic preaching.

————. *How to Preach to People's Needs.* Nashville: Abingdon Press, 1956.

Jackson sees preaching as a therapeutic tool. In each chapter he speaks of how to address a specific type of need such as loneliness or inferiority and then gives examples of how he and other preachers have preached to people in such need. Some of the outlines are helpful for the pastoral preacher.

Keck, Leander E. *The Bible in the Pulpit.* Nashville: Abingdon Press, 1978.

This book is a boon for the preacher who wants to be true to the biblical witness *and* speak to the deepest needs of modern men and women. Keck's idea of "priestly listening" unites the activities of pastor-student-preacher (pp. 62-63). He sees the New Testament writers as "pastoral theologians whose order in and shaping of the material were designed to confront their churches with a criticial word" (p. 96). Indeed the Bible shapes the content and the form of preaching. This is ably demonstrated in his three sermons included in the book.

Kemp, Charles F., ed. *Life-Situation Preaching.* St. Louis: Bethany Press, 1956.

This is primarily a sampling of some of the "pulpit greats'" pastoral sermons.

————, ed. *Pastoral Preaching.* St. Louis: Bethany Press, 1963.

This is the best of Kemp's books related to the area of pastoral theology and preaching. His definition on page twelve of pastoral preaching is most helpful. Also included in this volume are pastoral sermons delivered in various settings, such as hospitals, prisons, mental institutions.

————. *Physicians of the Soul.* New York: Macmillan, 1947.

This is not a deep book. Yet it is an interesting summary of the contributions of various leaders in the pastoral care movement including preachers who were also involved in pastoral counseling.

————, ed. *The Preaching Pastor.* St. Louis: Bethany Press, 1966.

This is similar to Dr. Kemp's other volumes on pastoral preaching. His theory of pastoral preaching is influenced and illustrated by Brooks, Jefferson, Fosdick, Farmer, and Quale. Their thinking is sprinkled throughout the introductory section. The collected pastoral sermons of preachers past and present address topics that go beyond the personal-problems emphasis.

An Annotated Bibliography

Killinger, John. *The Centrality of Preaching in the Total Task of the Ministry.* Waco, Tex.: Word Books, 1969.

His thesis that preaching and an adequate theology of preaching give one a center for the work of ministry (pp. 27-28) is an interesting viewpoint. The chapter on "Preaching and Pastoral Care" is most helpful and deals responsibly with the need to be servant of the Word and a servant of the people.

Linn, Edward Holt. *Preaching as Counseling.* Valley Forge, Pa.: Judson Press, 1966.

Harry E. Fosdick, after early frustration with the preaching task, hit upon the method later called "the counseling sermon." By Fosdick's own admission Linn seems to know "everything I ever did or said." So if you want Fosdick's technique and theology of life-situation preaching analyzed, this is the book.

Luccock, Halford E. *In the Minister's Workshop.* Nashville: Abingdon-Cokesbury Press, 1944.

This famous preacher and teacher of preaching devotes a large portion of this book to the merits and dangers of life-situation preaching. His view of a life-situation preacher as one kind of sermon does limit pastoral preaching to a "type" rather than a perspective for all preaching. Nonetheless there is much here that is beneficial and the dangers of one-sided pastoral preaching are clearly pointed out. To give but one example he shows the tendency to fail to call for repentance, individual and social, in "life-situation preaching" (pp. 86-88).

MacLennan, David A. *Pastoral Preaching.* Philadephia: The Westminster Press, 1955.

The largest portion of this book is devoted to resources and methods of pastoral preaching. This is not a very theological treatment, but tends to be more popular in its approach. Chapter 2 does contain a helpful list of objectives for preaching that is pastoral.

Mitchell, Henry H. *The Recovery of Preaching.* New York: Harper & Row, 1977.

Mitchell helps us "sit where they sit." He uses the resources of biblical stories, personal experience, and the preaching tradition of "Blackamerican" religion to forge a dialogical approach to preaching. Before reading this book I would have voted to retire the phrase, "preaching as dialogue," but Mitchell brings it alive through the black church experience.

Oates, Wayne. *The Christian Pastor*. Philadelphia: The Westminster Press, 1951.

This book includes a brief and sketchy treatment of "Preaching and the Pastoral Task." Of interest is his fourfold approach to "therapeutic preaching." One point deserves further study: therapeutic preaching "implies a conversational, eye-contact, extemporaneous delivery. . . ."

Oden, Thomas. *Kerygma and Counseling*. Philadelphia: The Westminster Press, 1966.

Oden uses self-disclosure (pp. 9, 16) as a theological bridge between proclamation and care-counseling. The chapter on "*Kerygma* or *Therapeia*" is thought provoking (pp. 146-70).

Pitt-Watson, Ian. *A Kind of Folly: Toward a Practical Theology of Preaching*. Edinburgh: Saint Andrew Press, 1976.

These Warrack lectures call for a double hermeneutic. The pastor-preacher must translate biblical theology into the language of contemporary experience. In addition he or she must hear in contemporary experience the living Word of God (p. 86). Pastoral preaching requires one to be at home in biblical and pastoral theology.

Skudlarek, William. *The Word in Worship: Preaching in a Liturgical Context*. Nashville: Abingdon Press, 1981.

There is so much of value here for the person who seeks to preach pastorally from the lectionary. When one has an understanding of the central purpose (pp. 28, 29) of the Roman Catholic lectionary of 1971 and the Protestant lectionaries based upon it, "the pastoral use of the lectionary" (chapter 3) is enhanced.

The appendix on aids to lectionary preaching is a valuable resource.

Smith, Charles W. F. *Biblical Authority for Modern Preaching*. Philadelphia: The Westminster Press, 1960.

This book could be easily overlooked as a resource for building a pastoral approach to preaching. To overlook this book would be to miss valuable insights on biblical preaching, the lectionary, and pastoral counseling. The titles of two chapters suggest the greatest contribution of the book: "The Claim of the Bible on the Preacher" and "The Claim of the People on the Preacher." The creative tension between these twin claims on us is powerfully presented by the author.

Steel, David. *Preaching Through the Year.* Atlanta: John Knox Press, 1980.

This is not a work laden with footnotes, but there is a lifetime of wisdom and pastoral practice behind it. David Steel gives practical suggestions for preaching through the church year for those who by tradition are not used to a lectionary. Even though this is done in a historical and theological context the tone is one of warmth and wit.

Steimle, Edmund A.; Niedenthel, Morris J.; and Rice, Charles L. *Preaching the Story.* Philadelphia: Fortress Press, 1980.

Although written as a general textbook on preaching, it makes several contributions to the study and practice of pastoral preaching. First, it includes a chapter on "Preaching in Pastoral Perspective" which gives a fine example of wrestling with a lectionary text, a personal problem, confidentiality, and the movement from the particular to the universal, all in the context of one sermon! The greatest overall contribution of the book is its emphasis on "balanced" preaching. The authors suggest that preaching needs an *image* or model which will mold each sermon (p. 11). "Storyteller" is the powerfully comprehensive image they develop. This is suggestive for pastoral preaching. Could it be that "shepherd" is a more comprehensive *image* than we have realized?

Switzer, David K. *Pastor, Preacher, Person: Developing a Pastoral Ministry in Depth.* Nashville: Abingdon Press, 1979.

Switzer is not afraid to think theologically about the pastoral ministry. A good example of that is his understanding of the church as the "Family of God." In building his ecclesiology on that image, he is able to draw from the social sciences aid in understanding and ministering to the family. Yet in this and his application of psychologist Carkuff's model of helping relationship to preaching he is careful not to let his psychology control his theology.

Teikmanis, Arthur L. *Preaching and Pastoral Care.* Philadelphia: Fortress Press, 1968.

The author follows the format established by Kemp and Jackson by using the first section of the book describing the relationship of preaching to pastoral care. The largest part of the book is given to illustrating pastoral preaching. This is not a particularly strong treatment of the topic.

Tizard, Leslie J. *Preaching; the Art of Communication.* New York: Oxford University Press, 1959.

Tizard's book addresses the possibility of "bringing the truth through personality." His last chapter on "Pastoral Preaching" deals primarily with what Killinger describes as "pre-counseling" in preaching. There is not much here beyond an elementary approach to empathetic preaching.

Volbeda, Samuel. *The Pastoral Genius of Preaching*. Grand Rapids: Zondervan Publishing House, 1960.

The peculiar character of authentic preaching is pastoral for this "very Reformed" author. The Bible is the book of pastoral care. The "double hermeneutic" of Ian Pitt-Watson becomes singular, or nearly so, with Volbeda. "We ministers of the post-apostolic age do not hear God speak to us. We only read what God has caused to be written" (pp. 38-39). He does echo the fullness of the shepherding model when he says preaching should be "feeding, guiding, protecting, and healing the sheep" (p. 125).

Watson, John (Ian Maclaren). *The Cure of Souls*. New York: Dodd, Mead, 1896.

This is a compendium of "pastoralia." We learn what books (theology and fiction) to read in 1896 and how big a church school room should be. Yet it does possess an enduring quality. For all its quaintness there is evidence of the high calling of the pastor-preacher to love and serve her or his people.

Willimon, William H. *Integrative Preaching: The Pulpit at the Center*. Nashville: Abingdon Press, 1981.

Willimon's well-reasoned argument for preaching at the center of pastoral ministry is reminiscent of John Killinger's book cited earlier. The significant difference is Willimon's emphasis on "the pastoral dimension of preaching as the inherently integrative quality of the preaching event. . . . While we are proclaiming the gospel in faithfulness and humility before the sacred text, we are also offering pastoral care to the people who stand before the text" (p. 21).

Articles

Bartlett, Gene E. "The Preaching and Pastoral Roles." *Pastoral Psychology* 6 (March 1952): 21-28.

This article seeks to show the role of preaching in helping people achieve mental health. It is constructive in its emphasis on "personmindedness." But Bartlett and others (i.e., Burns) writing in this issue seem almost embarrassed by such biblical concepts as judgment, responsibility, and repentance.

——. "When Preaching Becomes Real." *Pastoral Theology* 14 (October 1963): 17-25.

Bartlett brings together the dual needs of preaching: (1) a faith that God is acting in the sermon and (2) a *correspondence* of the words of God to the needs of people. "The listener too must feel he has been heard" (p. 22).

Burkhart, Roy A. "Preaching with Counseling Insight." *Pastoral Psychology* 8 (May 1957): 21-26.

There is here a good grasp of the "laboratories of experience" as commentaries on the text along with more "academic" commentaries.

Casteel, John L. "Homiletical Method for Pastoral Preaching" (Part I). *Pastoral Psychology* 6 (November 1955): 11-15.

In reading or hearing Casteel I am always impressed with his interdisciplinary approach. In this article he refuses to fall into the trap of seeing preaching as "group counseling." Yet he does suggest steps for building a sermon that is pastoral in its perspective.

——. "Homiletical Method for Pastoral Preaching," (Part II). *Pastoral Psychology* 6 (December 1955): 27-34.

Casteel here develops his homiletical steps in pastoral preaching: rapport, description, recognition, insight, and motivation.

Castner, Edward W. "A Theology of Ministry." *Drew Gateway* 47, No. 1 (1976-77): 55-71.

Castner applies an "Imaginative Theology" to the practice of ministry. There are some creative implications for preaching and pastoring in this.

Enright, William C. "Theology and the Crisis in the Pulpit." *Foundations* 18 (April-June 1975): 107-14.

The author suggests a theological process for preaching: biblical orientation, christological, soteriological, contemporary, and *pastoral*. He quotes von Allman concerning the necessity of preaching being a part of pastoral work (p. 114).

Farmer, Herbert H. "The Preacher and Persons." *Review and Expositor* 43 (Oct. 1946): 403-18.

A theologian gives an eloquent plea for the pastoral perspective in preaching. He uses the Christian understanding of love as a way of presenting the need to make truth personal.

Fosdick, Harry E. "The Preacher and Persons." *Pastoral Psychology* 2 (March 1952): 11-15.

This article makes clear Fosdick's preaching method of beginning with people's needs. There is a high respect here for the "human documents" in preparing and delivering sermons (p. 12). Fosdick also gives some criticisms of his own method (p. 14).

Glick, J. D. "Confessional Preaching." *The Christian Ministry* 8 (September 1977): 25-29.

The author, a Brethren minister, gives some practical guidelines for confessional preaching *and* worship that draw people into a potentially therapeutic atmosphere. The article would be strengthened by mention of some dangers in the confessional approach.

Horne, Chevis. "What Is Pastoral Preaching?" *Search* 9 (Winter 1977): 51-54.

This is one of the very few articles on pastoral preaching written in the past ten to fifteen years. Horne carries forward general themes that marked the literature of pastoral counseling in the 1950s and early 1960s. The emphasis is on pastoral preaching being accepting, supportive, and nurturing. More about the nurturing aspect: "speaking the truth in love" would have been welcomed. Horne sees pastoral preaching as the foundation for evangelistic and prophetic preaching.

Hudson, R. Lofton. "Preaching and Mental Health." *Pastoral Psychology* 14 (October 1963): 33-39.

A call for empathetic understanding within the context of proclamation is the focus of this article.

———. "Therapeutic Preaching." *Review and Expositor* 49 (July 1952): 292-303.

There are some good insights here for preaching that heals and gives life. Yet I am bothered by his seeing some *subjects* as not very conducive to therapeutic preaching while others are. Is it not a question more of perspective than theme?

Keller, Roger. "The Lectionary: Straightjacket or Coat of Many Colors?" *The Duke Divinity School Review* 44 (Winter 1979): 49-53.

Here is an all too rare argument for the pastoral value of preaching from the lectionary. The term "pastoral" is not used but Keller concludes "that in the course of a year far more human joys, sorrows, hopes and fears, problems and situations are dealt with through lectionary preaching" than in other methods of preaching (p. 52).

Kemp, Charles F. "Life-Situation Preaching and Pastoral Work." *Pastoral Psychology* 7 (October 1956): 35-46.
The strong point of this article is that pastoral care and preaching must be "life situational" to inform and *shape* each other.

Kirkland, William H. "Priest and Prophet." *The Pulpit* 20 (November 1955): 2-5.
Don't let the length of the article mislead you. Here are some very sound theological-biblical guidelines for developing the priestly and the prophetic aspects of pastoral preaching.

Long, Thomas G. "Therapeutic Preaching: Three Views." *The Princeton Seminary Bulletin* 68 (Winter 1976): 82-93.
This is an important article in that three views of therapeutic preaching are compared and analyzed. The views are those of Welsh, Davis, and Menninger. He finds all three have an inadequate view of therapy and kerygma as they are related to preaching.

Mueller, Charles S. "Pastoral Preaching in the Parish." *Concordia Theological Monthly* 42 (February 1979): 117-23.
A Lutheran speaks out of a rich pastoral tradition to put an emphasis on the pastoral relationship and community spirit possible within the parish context.

Starenko, Ronald C. "Preaching and Counseling." *Concordia Theological Monthly* 42 (October 1971): 633-37.
Starenko effectively shows the danger of a false dichotomy between counseling and preaching that forces pastors to choose between them. While celebrating their differences he seeks to show their relationships.

Tillich, Paul. "Communicating the Gospel." *Pastoral Psychology* 7 (June 1956): 10-16.
Tillich gives a fairly clear summary of his view of preaching that includes an emphasis on preaching to the needs of individuals and of society. This is done without trying to remove the "stumbling block" of the gospel. However, Tillich wisely reminds us that we may erect our own stumbling blocks and confuse these with the "offense of the gospel."

Watkins, Keith. "Protestants Rediscover the Word?" *Worship* 53 (March 1979): 119-25.

Dr. Watkins sees the importance of an objective reference in worship provided by the sensitive, intelligent use of the lectionary. Such use keeps preaching from becoming "a kind of pep session for the good life" (p. 124).

Wood, Frederick C., Jr. "Kerygma and Therapy: The Pastor's Dilemma." *Union Seminary Quarterly Review* 18 (January 1963): 123-34.

This is an excellent article dealing with the relationship of the saving and healing aspects of the gospel as they show themselves in the preached Word.

Dissertations and Theses

(A listing of some theses related to pastoral preaching)

Albright, Edwin W. "Pastoral Preaching." Th.M., Louisville Presbyterian Seminary, 1954.

Fenton, Donald R. "Preaching in the Pastoral Context." D.Min., Southern Methodist University, 1974.

Boyer, Ralph A., III. "Interrelatedness of Pastoral Counseling and Preaching with Special Emphasis upon the Ministries of the Rev. Dr. Harry Emerson Fosdick and the Rev. Dr. Leslie Dixon Weatherhead." Ph.D., Temple University, 1960.

Coburn, Kimball Boyd, Sr. "Prophetic Preaching from a Pastoral Base." D.Min., the School of Theology at Claremont, 1975.

Crawford, Allen P. "The Minister's Function in Preaching and Counseling." M.A., Union Theological Seminary, 1947.

Dye, Leslie E. "A Study of Relationships Between Preaching and Pastoral Counseling." M.S., Christian Theological Seminary, 1954.

Harrel, Douglas. "The Relationship of Life Situation Preaching to Pastoral Counseling." D.Min., The School of Theology at Claremont, 1976.

Hatch, Leonard J. "Lay Contributions to Sermon Preparation." D.Min., Eastern Baptist Theological Seminary, 1976.

Heetland, David Lee. "Toward an Interpersonal Theory of Preaching." Th.D., The Iliff School of Theology, 1975.

Hult, Dertil E. "The Relationship of Counseling and Preaching." Th.M., Harvard Divinity School, 1958.

An Annotated Bibliography

Johnson, R. V. "Biblical Preaching and Its Relationship to Counseling." M.Th., Northern Baptist Seminary, 1962.

McDiarmid, A. B. "A Critique of H. E. Fosdick's Conception of Preaching as Personal Counselling on a Group Scale." Th.D., Pacific School of Religion, 1961.

Meux, Joseph Clay. "The Power of Healing Found in the Christian Pulpit Through the Centuries." S.T.M., Vanderbilt Divinity School, 1967.

Moseley, Danny. "The Pastoral and Prophetic Roles in the Ministry of Reconciliation." D.D., The Divinity School of Vanderbilt University, 1970.

Reid, Clyde H. "Two-Way Communication Through Small Groups in Relation to Preaching." Th.D., Boston University School of Theology, 1960.

Ritzinger, Lynney B., Jr. "A Study of Pastoral Care in the Lyman Beecher Lectures." Ph.D., Southwestern Baptist Theological Seminary, 1958.

Rothaar, Michael Robert. "Person-Centered Preaching: Developing Small Lay Study Groups on Weekly Pericopes as Part of the Process of Sermon Preparation." D.Min., Drew University, 1980.

Shealy, Wilburn Ross. "The Power of the Present: The Pastoral Perspective of Richard Baxter Puritan Divine: 1615-1691." Ph.D., Drew University, 1966.

Steere, David A. "A New Pastoral Theology: A Study of Its Redefinition in the Clinical Pastoral Education Movement According to the Biblical Concept of Shepherding." Th.D., Union Theological Seminary, 1966.

Wilburn, John M., Jr. "The Relationship of Pastoral Counseling to Preaching." S.T.M., Andover-Newton Theological School, 1952.

NOTES

Chapter I—Pastoral Preaching: The Truth in Love

1. Frederick Buechner, *The Final Beast* (New York: The Seabury Press, 1967), p. 28.
2. Herbert H. Farmer, *The Servant of the Word* (Philadelphia: Fortress Press, 1964), p. 15.
3. Phillips Brooks, *Eight Lectures on Preaching* (London: S.P.C.K., 1959), pp. 5, 7.
4. Frederick C. Wood, Jr., "Kerygma and Therapy: The Pastor's Dilemma," *Union Seminary Quarterly Review* 18 (January 1963), 123.
5. Frederick Buechner, *Telling the Truth: The Gospel as Tragedy, Comedy, and Fairy Tale* (New York: Harper & Row, 1977), p. 8.
6. Farmer, *The Servant of the Word,* p. 66. (Emphasis my own.)
7. Georges Bernanos, *The Diary of a Country Priest,* trans. Pamela Morris (New York: Macmillan, 1937), p. 54.
8. Farmer, *The Servant of the Word,* p. 46.
9. For more on these two concepts see the annotated bibliography, especially works by and about H. E. Fosdick and Seward Hiltner.
10. Seward Hiltner, *The Christian Shepherd: Some Aspects of Pastoral Care* (Nashville: Abingdon Press, 1959), p. 20.

Chapter II—The Biblical Image of Shepherd

1. David Alden Steere, "A New Pastoral Theology: A Study of Its Redefinition in the Clinical Pastoral Education Movement According to the Biblical Concept of Shepherding" (Th.D. diss., Union Theological Seminary, 1966), p. 44.
2. Ronald E. Osborn, *In Christ's Place: Christian Ministry in Today's World* (St. Louis: Bethany Press, 1967), p. 119.
3. John F. Jansen, "The Pastoral Image in the New Testament," *Austin Seminary Bulletin* XCIV (May 1979), 14-15.
4. Steere, "A New Pastoral Theology," pp. 84-93.
5. Hiltner, *The Christian Shepherd,* p. 20.
6. Steere, "A New Pastoral Theology," p. 87.
7. *Ibid.,* p. 88.
8. See David E. Babin, *Week In-Week Out: A New Look at Liturgical Preaching* (New York: The Seabury Press, 1976). Also an important book on the pastoral perspective in worship is William H. Willimon, *Worship as Pastoral Care* (Nashville: Abingdon Press, 1979).
9. Philip B. Taft, Jr., "Sojourners: Angry Prophets to Loving Critics," *A.D. 1979* 8 (September 1979), 26-28.
10. This address was delivered at the Riverside Church in New York

during the "Harry Emerson Fosdick Ecumenical Convocation on Preaching," October 19, 1978.

11. Steere, "A New Pastoral Theology," p. 88.

12. For more on this idea of being priests to one another see Carlyle Marney, *Priests to Each Other* (Valley Forge, Pa.: Judson Press, 1974), pp. 7-16.

13. Ralph L. Underwood, "Pastoral Care and the Office of the Pastor," *Austin Seminary Bulletin* XCIV (May 1979), 6.

14. Hiltner, *The Christian Shepherd*, p. 14.

15. Rudolf Bohren, *Preaching and Community*, trans. David E. Green (Atlanta: John Knox Press, 1966), pp. 110-11.

16. *Ibid.*

17. Richard Baxter, *The Reformed Pastor* (Grand Rapids: Sovereign Grace Press, 1971), p. 1.

18. *Ibid.,* p. 11.

19. Robert S. Paul, *Ministry* (Grand Rapids: Eerdmans Publishing Co., 1965), pp. 187-88.

20. Peter Berger, *Facing Up to Modernity* (New York: Basic Books, 1977), p. 186.

21. Jorge Lara-Braud and Jeanne Audrey Powers, "Paper on Ministry" (Consultation on Church Union for Task Force of Women, March 9-10, 1978), p. 2.

22. Don S. Browning, *The Moral Context of Pastoral Care* (Philadelphia: The Westminster Press, 1976) offers a brief summary of these modes on page 25. For a more complete survey: William A. Clebsch and Charles R. Jaekle, *Pastoral Care in Historical Perspective* (Englewood Cliffs, N.J.: Prentice-Hall, 1964).

23. Charles E. Jefferson, *The Minister as Shepherd* (New York: Thomas Y. Crowell, 1912), p. 83. For a description of Jefferson's seven elements of the Shepherd's work see pp. 48-83.

24. *Ibid.,* p. 54.

25. *Ibid.,* pp. 55-56.

26. Browning, *The Moral Context of Pastoral Care*, p. 103.

27. Thomas C. Oden, *Agenda for Theology* (New York: Harper & Row, 1979), pp. 97, 102.

28. *Ibid.,* pp. 15, 99, 101, 104.

29. *Ibid.,* pp. 76-78, 105.

30. John T. McNeill, *A History of the Cure of Souls* (New York: Harper & Brothers, 1951, paperback ed., 1977), p. 100.

Chapter III—Telling the Whole Truth

1. Paul Scherer, *For We Have This Treasure: The Yale Lectures on Preaching, 1943* (Grand Rapids: Baker Book House, 1976), p. 70.

2. I am indebted to Dr. Peggy Way for the suggestion that a "pastoral moment" is truthful, helpful, and imaginative.

3. David K. Switzer, *Pastor, Preacher, Person: Developing a Pastoral Ministry in Depth* (Nashville: Abingdon Press, 1979), pp. 70-95.

4. Urban T. Holmes, *Ministry and Imagination* (New York: The Seabury Press, 1976), pp. 232, 88, 87.

5. John Calvin, *Calvin's Commentaries: The Acts of the Apostles, 14-28*, trans. John W. Fraser (Edinburgh: Oliver and Boyd, 1966), p. 18.

6. James D. Smart, *The Strange Silence of the Bible in the Church: A Study in Hermeneutics* (Philadelphia: The Westminster Press, 1970), p. 164.

7. Switzer, *Pastor, Preacher, Person*, p. 101. Switzer points out that this expression was borrowed from Nietzsche.

8. Leander E. Keck, *The Bible in the Pulpit* (Nashville: Abingdon Press, 1978), p. 62.

9. Lecture delivered by Dr. Read at the "Tennessee Convocation on Preaching," in Nashville, on April 24, 1979.

10. Carl E. Braaten, *The Whole Counsel of God* (Philadelphia: Fortress Press, 1974), p. ix.

11. Brooks, *Eight Lectures on Preaching*, p. 90.

12. Harry Emerson Fosdick, *The Living of These Days* (New York: Harper & Brothers, 1956), p. 92.

13. Roger Keller, "The Lectionary: Straightjacket or Coat of Many Colors?" *The Duke Divinity School Review* 44 (Winter 1979), 52.

14. Charles Williams, *The New Christian Year* (Toronto: Oxford University Press, 1941), p. v. Another valuable resource of the wisdom of "teachers and saints" ordered according to the Christian Year is George Forell's two-volume work: *The Christian Year* (Nashville: Thomas Nelson, 1965).

15. Brian McCarthy, "Two Cheers for the Three-Year Lectionary," *The Christian Ministry* XI, 2 (March 1980), 36.

16. George E. Sweazey, *Preaching the Good News* (Englewood Cliffs, N.J.: Prentice-Hall, 1976), p. 48. Sweazey admits his questions come from one who has not used the lectionary. (See page 65.)

Chapter IV—The Practice of Pastoral Preaching

1. Charles Jefferson, *Quiet Hints to Growing Preachers* (New York: Thomas Y. Crowell, 1901), pp. 199-200.

2. This description of my approach to indirect preparation is taken from a previously published article: Gary Stratman, "Of Preaching and Preparation," *Church Management: The Clergy Journal* LII, 6 (April 1976), 27-29. The essay referred to is found in Francis Bacon, *Selected Writings*, ed. Hugh G. Dick (New York: Random House, 1955), pp. 128-29.

3. William Barclay, *William Barclay: A Spiritual Autobiography* (Grand Rapids: Eerdmans Publishing Co., 1975), p. 84.

4. After my initial reading of the text I find Reginald Fuller's work helpful: *Preaching the New Lectionary: The Word of God for the Church Today* (Collegeville, Minn.: Liturgical Press, 1974).

5. Peter Taylor Forsyth, *Positive Preaching and the Modern Mind* (Grand Rapids: Eerdmans Publishing Co., 1964), pp. 281-82.

6. Heije Faber and Ebel van der Schoot, *The Art of Pastoral Conversation* (Nashville: Abingdon Press, 1965), p. 175.

Notes for Pages 62-72

7. From William Law's *Letters* quoted in Williams, *The New Christian Year*, p. 190.

8. Daniel Day Williams, *The Minister and the Care of Souls* (New York: Harper & Brothers, 1961, reprint, 1977), p. 121.

9. If one or two of the other lectionary texts are used, the key exegetical notes are included at the top of the worksheet.

10. Gustave Frenssen confided:

My text so to speak saunters up and down the village streets once or twice with thoughtful eyes and meditative mind. It becomes accustomed to the village, learns to feel at home in it. . . . As I write, I deliberately address certain definite people. . . . And so I feel that my sermons are firmly rooted in actual life, that each of them has a certain amount of strength, a certain power to quicken and inspire.

Quoted by Scherer, *For We Have This Treasure*, p. 156.

11. Charles Reynolds Brown, *The Art of Preaching* (New York: Macmillan, 1922), p. 84.

12. Wayne Oates, *The Christian Pastor* (Philadelphia: The Westminster Press, 1951), p. 68. (I do not believe Oates' use of the word "extemporaneous" here implies "unplanned." Rather this style of preaching demands a great deal in the way of preparation.)

Chapter V—Three Pastoral Sermons

1. Farmer, *The Servant of the Word*, p. 66.
2. *Ibid.*